STATELY PROGRESS

ROYAL TRAIN TRAVEL
SINCE 1840

Amba Kumar

NATIONAL RAILWAY MUSEUM

In memory of my dearest mother, my beautiful
angel, Shobha Kumari

11 October 1949 – 8 July 1997

Your ways were ways of gentleness and all your
paths were peace.

From your loving Rani

Said the child

I love you . . .

I shall love you as long as you live

And when you are dead

I shall love you as long as I live

And when I am dead

I shall love you as long as God lives . . .

CONTENTS

ACKNOWLEDGEMENTS

I would like to express my grateful thanks for the gracious permission of Her Majesty the Queen to make use of material contained in the Royal Archives, and thanks to Jill Kelsey, Assistant Registrar. Thanks also to the Royal Borough Collection, The Royal Borough of Windsor and Maidenhead for permission to quote from the diaries of Samuel Maun, and to Joan Grundy for permission to quote from Fred Beeken's interview. Especial thanks to Chris Hillyard, Royal Train Foreman, for his kind and thoughtful support to me during the writing of this book, and to Norman Pattenden MBE, Royal Train Officer. I would also like to thank: Patrick Kingston for his time, advice and generous provision of material; Brian Morrison, Paul Whiting, Leslie Charlesworth, David Lunn and Inspector Michael Foster of British Transport Police for permissions to use photographs; Sir William McAlpine Bt; *Railnews*; Damian Eaton of Great Yarmouth Museums; and my mother for her encouragement, support and advice in this and in all things.

There are also staff members at the National Railway Museum (NRM) and the Science Museum whom I would like to thank, beginning with Andrew Scott, Head of the NRM, for giving me this, my first book, to write in 1995. Thanks also go to: Anna Hodson, Giskin Day and my wonderful editor, Nicholas Stead, of the Publications Unit at the Science Museum; Lynn Patrick and John Perkin of the NRM photographic studio; Dieter Hopkin; Tony Filby; Phil Atkins, who made comments and suggestions as I wrote the book; and Ed Bartholomew, who did the same, and who carried heavy volumes up and down long flights of stairs for me. I would also like to thank Mike Blakemore who gave the book its title, and Debbie Heron who transcribed almost indecipherable taped interviews so patiently.

Finally, I would like to acknowledge the contribution made to this book by the Science & Society Picture Library at the Science Museum.

INTRODUCTION

The ancients chronicled, with wonder and fascination, the majesty of Cleopatra's fabled golden barge. Today's chroniclers write with equal amazement and exaggeration about Queen Elizabeth II's Royal Train. Their tabloid reports weave a web of fiction around the Royal Train, inciting speculation, reverence, envy and trenchant criticism. Paradoxically, however, few authors have paid any attention to the real significance it has played in the lives of the British Royal Family.

The lavish furnishings of the Victorian and Edwardian Royal Trains caused them to be dubbed 'palaces on wheels'. Two world wars and the changing needs of the Royal Family have caused the Royal Train to evolve into a palace on wheels in its practical sense. Today, it facilitates the fulfilment of royal public duties by carrying the Royal Family to almost any part of the realm, whilst providing it with a home-away-from-home, permitting the affairs of the nation to be continued without interruption.

The evocative exhibition of royal saloons at the National Railway Museum, which this book complements, spans the period from 1840 to 1977, and the progression from the silken blue splendour of Queen Victoria's carriage to the more austere lines of the old wartime saloon of Queen Elizabeth, the Queen Mother is strongly marked.

The last 150 years have also seen the evolution of a small but dedicated body of staff whose function is to manage the running of the train. Its members go mostly unremarked, but their close association with the Royal Train has been the seeding ground for some entertaining and insightful anecdotes. It is the aim of this book to use these anecdotes and documentary evidence to show how, since 1840, the Royal Train has drawn together the panoply of state affairs and the domestic lives and aesthetic tastes of the Royal Family in a unique and remarkable combination.

QUEEN ADELAIDE
royal rail pioneer

'A most prosperous and quick journey'

In 1840, Queen Adelaide, Princess of Saxe-Meiningen, widow of King William IV of England, and aunt to the recently crowned Queen Victoria, made a tour of the northern provinces of England by rail. She was the first monarch of England to use the new technology. It was a mode of conveyance so revolutionary that it was described as the 'magician's road'.

At the time that Queen Adelaide made her historic journey, railways were just beginning to carve their way through England. In past centuries, if monarchs wished to tour the realm, their numerous household staff members, with wagonloads of luggage, including furniture, would have to accompany them. The entourage would have been composed of a large number of carriages and horses, as well as a mounted troop of guards to provide the event with both the expected pageantry and the necessary security. For the Royal Household to travel was, therefore, a massive and cumbersome undertaking. Steam locomotion made it possible for the Royal Family to travel to different parts of the country more easily and frequently, and to be seen by those of their subjects who had never had the opportunity to travel to London.

A discreet note in the Court Circular in *The Times* of 20 July 1840 states that,

Her Majesty the Queen Dowager accompanied by the Duchess Ida of Saxe-Weimar arrived in town on Saturday morning from Bushy-park. Her Majesty, attended by her Suite, went to the station of the London and Birmingham Railway in Boston square, and left by a special train at half-past 10 o'clock, attended by the Earl and Countess of Sheffield and the Earl of Denbigh for the seat of the Earl of Brownlow, Belton House, Grantham.

It appears that the event was marked with little pomp and celebration, its occurrence reported as though it were quite usual for the Royal Family to travel several hundred miles to the Midlands to visit friends.

Despite this lack of occasion, Adelaide's journey did set the precedent for every single succeeding royal train journey to the present day, because of the splendid carriage provided for her use. The London & Birmingham Railway had been selected to provide Queen Adelaide with a saloon. They presented her with the most up-to-date carriage that current technology could produce, a practice which is still maintained today. Victoria's cousin, King Ernest Augustus of Hanover, later inspected Adelaide's carriage and was so impressed that he ordered a replica for his personal use.

Unlike Victoria, Adelaide was not a prolific correspondent and keeper of journals, but she was on close and affectionate terms with her young niece. She wrote to Victoria on 20 July

Queen Adelaide.
NRM 161/95

Opposite: Queen Adelaide's saloon, built in 1842, pictured here at the NRM. Its construction clearly shows the influence of stage coach design on the new railway industry. *NRM CT970144*

from Belton House to tell her about this exciting new experience:

We had a most prosperous and quick journey and were only ten hours on the road from Bushy to this place. We left home at half past eight o'clock and stopt half an hour at Leicester on leaving the Railroad from which place we posted on with horses instead of steam to this most comfortable and beautifully furnished house . . . . My sister [Duchess Ida] did not feel quite well after the Railroad Expedition, it made her almost *sea sick*.[1]

Queen Adelaide's saloon, arranged for night accommodation. A cushion placed between the seats and a raised flap, opening up a connecting boot, allowed her to lie down.
NRM 185/92

Despite Ida's motion sickness, Adelaide's first train journey appears to have been one she remembered with pleasure, and she recognised the advantages the railways offered. It was to be another two years before Victoria herself made her first journey by train. She was famously resistant to changes and new ways, but the glowing report of rail travel sent to her by her aunt must have taken root in her mind. The Great Western Railway (GWR) had also been watching which way the wind was blowing. Now that the railways had been granted royal favour it quietly went to work, determined to be the first to claim the grand prize: the honour of conveying Queen Victoria.

Northchurch Tunnel during construction of the London & Birmingham Railway in the 1830s.
The first British royal journey by train was made on this line.

QUEEN VICTORIA
the customer is always right

'I am quite charmed by it'

'We arrived here yesterday morn. having come by the rail-road from Windsor, in half an hour free from dust and crowd, & heat, & I am quite charmed by it'[1], wrote Queen Victoria to her uncle, King Leopold of Belgium, of her first journey by train on 13 June 1842. In her journal she enthused further:

At 1/2 p[ast].11 we left Windsor, which we were very sorry to do, in this fine weather. We drove to the Slough station . . .. The saloon we travelled in on the train was very large and beautifully fitted up. It took us exactly 30 minutes going to Paddington, & the motion was very slight, & much easier than a carriage, also no dust or great heat—in fact, it was delightful, & so quick. We were at Buckingham Palace by 20 m[inutes]. to 1.[2]

Victoria, entranced by her experience, became a firm convert to the new cause. Her delight sprung from her realisation that she could now travel long distances without facing the ordeal of noisy, staring crowds lining her route. Although the railways had ventured into the realm of passenger travel with the opening of the Stockton & Darlington Railway in 1825, they were still regarded with some suspicion, and royal patronage gave them a stamp of respectability.

Baroness Lehzen, who had been Victoria's autocratic and influential governess, was clearly impressed by the juggernaut qualities of the railways, for her notepaper was embossed with a golden engine and the inscription 'I am coming'. However, it was the Prince Consort, Albert, who probably persuaded his doting new wife to take the train back to London that June morning. He was interested in new forms of technology and had taken his first train journey in 1839, when he and his brother, Ernest, had been courting Victoria together.

The message from Windsor had come at very short notice on Saturday 11 June, just two days before the train was required. Several companies owned the routes out of London and all were vying for the first royal passengers, but the GWR had lain in wait, ready to produce the royal saloon it had constructed in 1840. The interior was royally upholstered in crimson and white silk, the furniture was in the style of Louis XIV, and paintings by Parris of the 'Four Elements' hung on the walls. After receiving the notice from the Palace, the GWR hastily assembled a train of six carriages led by the engine *Phlegethon*.

The royal party were met at Slough station by various important officials of the GWR. A reporter for *The Times* noted that the delay necessitated by the loading of these vehicles at the start of the journey in Windsor enabled a fascinated, and perhaps a little apprehensive, Victoria to proceed to the line where she, 'examined the Royal Saloon, inquiring very minutely into the whole of the arrangements'..

Opposite: A drawing of Queen Victoria, Prince Albert and their young children departing for Scotland in about 1850. *BTF 9648*

This strange new beast mesmerised other members of the Royal Household too. Victoria's Master of the Horse inspected the station and the train some hours before the journey, while her coachman invited himself to ride on the footplate so that he could play with the engine's controls during the trip itself. At exactly 12.00 p.m. the train departed, driven by two of the most famous personalities in railway history, Daniel Gooch, principal of the GWR locomotive department and designer of the *Phlegethon,* and Isambard Kingdom Brunel, chief engineer of the GWR.

In the meantime, there had been bustling preparations at Paddington. Part of the platform had been made secure and covered with a crimson carpet 'which reached from one end of the platform to the other'[4]. Arrangements were timed almost to the second. At precisely 11.55 a.m., the Queen's carriage, drawn by four horses, arrived from the Royal Mews at Pimlico in readiness to convey her to Buckingham Palace. It was closely followed by Captain Sir G Brown and a detachment of the 8th Royal Hussars from the barracks at Kensington, who were to provide Victoria with an escort. The Royal Train arrived at 12.25 p.m. Albert dismounted first, and helped Victoria out of the saloon. They were met by more high-ranking officials, led by senior members of the Metropolitan Police. *The Times* reported that on alighting from the train, the Queen 'was received with the most deafening demonstrations of loyalty and affection we have ever experienced'[5]. Unfortunately, not all the

Victoria and Albert arrive at King's Cross Station in 1851, ready to embark on their tour of the north of England. The carriage was built specially for them by the Great Northern Railway. *445/97*

characters who took part in this historic journey had such a pleasant time: the coachman who had ridden on the footplate had so dirtied his scarlet livery, that he was discouraged from ever repeating his experience again.

Running the Royal Train

If the arrangements for the inaugural journey of the Queen were undertaken so exactingly, then the preparations which went into the subsequent running of the Royal Train were planned with mathematical precision, and executed with the attention to detail usually accorded to a military campaign. A 'Special Notice', showing where the Royal Train was intended to be at any given time and location during the journey, would be printed, marked 'Private—for the use of staff concerned only'. There were also *Standard Instructions for Working Royal Trains* (in place by 1861) which obliged the Locomotive Superintendent to 'select the Engines and take every precaution to secure the most perfect class suited to the nature of the Train so as to avoid any possibility of failure or delay: he will also select the Enginemen for the Royal Train (and for the Pilot Engine) from the most steady and experienced drivers who know the road well'[6]. This 'pilot engine' was employed to run ten minutes ahead of the Royal Train, the theory being that if there were any problems with security hazards, the pilot engine would take the brunt, and still leave enough time to warn the oncoming Royal Train. In these early days of rail travel, when signalling and track operations were rather temperamental, the stationmasters along the line would have to personally oversee that the switches for points on the track were correctly set, and then locked down until both the pilot engine and the Royal Train had passed. At the end of the journey, the pilot

Queen Victoria crosses the Tay Bridge in Dundee, 1897. Later that year, the bridge was destroyed in a violent storm, taking a passenger train with it into the river. *346/92*

engine would be diverted off the main line so that the Royal Train could coast into the station.

The railway companies' involvement with the smooth running of the Royal Train did not end with the operation of the machinery. It became the unaltered custom for the Royal Train to receive personal supervision from the highest ranking officers, who would usually leave such tasks to the more junior members of the organisation on more prosaic occasions. The 'artificers' of the rolling stock (officials from the company who had built the saloon) would travel with the train over the 'foreign' lines of other companies, and would be responsible for the sound performance and overall fitness of the vehicle. The operation of the train and the train itself would be in the charge of a senior operating officer employed by the company over whose line the train was travelling. Where the track changed over to another company, other officials would join the train. Two travelling inspectors would assume the duties of the guard, and the senior of the two would keep a record of all those travelling, probably so that fares could be raised later with the Royal Household.

The arrival of the Royal Train also required precise arrangements. The *Standard Instructions*

Queen Victoria and Princess Henry of Battenberg travel through the South of France in the Queen's continental saloons in 1892. They sit in the drawing room, decorated in blue, yellow, white and grey silks.
448/97

dictated that a chalk mark, which could be easily distinguished, should be made on the platform, and that a man with a red flag should stand by it and indicate to the driver where the footplate should be once the train had stopped. On occasion, things could go wrong: G P Neele, the Locomotive Superintendent of the London & North Western Railway (LNWR) recorded in his *Railway Reminiscences* (1904) that,

the Great Western officer . . . 'cut' the train in the wrong place with the result that the saloon conveying the ladies-in-waiting was taken to a platform remote from the Queen's waiting room, and they were unable to find their

way back in time to take up their expected places . . . such an impression was made that even twelve months afterwards I was reminded by the ladies of the *contretemps*.[7]

Railways and relaxation

Victoria delighted in the advantages afforded by train travel, not least the time it allowed her for rest and relaxation. Her journal entry for 23 November 1880 records her enjoyment of Charlotte Bronte's *Jane Eyre*. It was 'a wonderful book, very peculiar in parts, but so powerfully and admirably written'[8]. The Queen was also very fond of card games, in particular

Queen Victoria and Prince Albert dismount from the South Eastern Railway saloon at Gosport Station, on the occasion of the state visit by Louis Philippe, King of France, in 1844. The King helps the Queen down the steps, the Duke of Wellington (holding feathered hat) stands by. *BTC 469/53*

Model at 1/16 scale of the LNWR royal saloon constructed for Queen Victoria in 1869. It shows how the carriage was originally designed to be a pair of saloons, for day and night use. *NRM CT970140*

Brass footwarmer from the GWR royal saloon, used from about 1860 to 1901. Filled with hot water it would only remain warm for a few hours. Alternatives were footwarmers which had been immersed in boiling water and then filled with acetate of soda crystals. The resulting chemical reaction would provide heat for up to 60 hours. *NRM CT970134*

'Patience'. In later years, it became her favourite game and she had a specially made 'Patience table' installed in her carriage.

In 1846, Victoria and Albert purchased Osborne House on the Isle of Wight as a private retreat. The Queen would continue to visit Osborne until the end of her life, but the island was untouched by the railways until 1862, when a private station was constructed at Whippingham, close to the house, at Victoria's request. In 1888, the Queen took a ride on the newly opened Isle of Wight Railway, but her journal entry for 11 February reveals her to have been slightly unimpressed by the experience. She felt that 'the carriage was not uncomfortable, but the line is not very well laid, & winding . . .. The station at Ventnor is a small one.'[9]

If Albert was the first love of Victoria's life, then in the Highlands of Scotland in 1848 she met the second: Balmoral Castle. Victoria would holiday there each year until her death. In 1848, the easiest way for a royal entourage to travel this far from London would be to use the Royal

Yacht, but the railways were just beginning to inch into the northernmost points of the country. Victoria had made plans to sail back from Scotland to London, but the morning of Friday 29 September dawned wet and foggy, making it impossible for the party to attempt the journey. The Aberdeen Railway hastily cobbled together a Royal Train from ordinary first-class carriages, and Victoria and Albert set off for London. It took the combined efforts of six companies over two days to take the Queen and Prince Consort back to England, but they had proved their worth to the Royal Family yet again. From now on, the Queen's Scottish sojourns would begin by rail. Neele records the journey to Balmoral on 29 August 1859. The Royal Family travelled overnight from Kings Cross Station, stopping at Biggleswade, Peterborough, Newark and Doncaster. They reached Edinburgh at 8.00 a.m. the next day, where they were joined by the Prince of Wales. They then used the Edinburgh & Glasgow Railway to get to Larbert Junction, where the train changed over to the Scottish Central Railway lines which took them to Perth. There, the Scottish North Eastern Railway took the baton until Aberdeen was reached. The royal party was escorted on the final stage of their journey by the directors of the Deeside Railway, which owned the last miles of track to Banchory, then the closest station to Balmoral. Throughout the journey, the Queen would occupy her LNWR saloon, despite the fact that she was travelling over lines belonging to several different companies. As the railway system improved, the journey to Scotland became less tortuous, helped by the fact that in 1866 a station was built at Ballater village near Balmoral.

For centuries, it had been the custom for monarchs to tour the realm and be seen by their subjects, staying at the great houses of the nobility on the way. Now that the railways had made it infinitely easier for this particular queen to travel, Victoria's household could be fitted

neatly inside six carriages. G P Neele described the scene at Derby on 21 May 1891: 'The passage of the Queen's train by daylight was an entirely new thing to the inhabitants of this district, and the crowds to catch sight of it and perchance of Her Majesty were very great. The Midland Company decorated their station at Derby with much taste; it was a very artistic display.'[10] In 1849 and 1861, Victoria and Albert used the LNWR to travel the long distance to Holyhead, and thence sailed on a tour to Ireland where they visited Dublin. Occasionally, the Queen would also venture across the Channel to France. If so, she would travel in a pair of six-wheeled saloons, French-built, but very similar to her LNWR vehicles of the time.

The Royal Train also made itself useful by helping to continue the ancient custom of state visits by foreign royalty to a reigning monarch. During her long reign, Victoria was hostess to hordes of visiting royalty, from all parts of the globe. On 4 June 1887, Kapiolani, Queen of the Sandwich Islands (in the South Pacific), together with her sister Liliokilani, visited England. At Rugby Station, they caught sight of a little girl holding a large bundle of may blossom in her arms. Enchanted by the strange flowers, so unlike anything which grew in her homelands, Queen Kapiolani made a request to Neele, Superintendent of the LNWR, for some of the blooms. In return, Neele requested her to sign his 'birthday book', but Liliokilani signed it on her sister's behalf, telling him that she always wrote for Queen Kapiolani as she was more skilled than her in the art of writing.

Wooden commode with decorated bowl in Victoria's toilet compartment adjoining her LNWR day saloon. The walls in this room are hung with blue brocade and silk to match the day compartment. *NRM T937417*

17

The Queen is not amused: Victoria and the railway companies

Albert, Prince Consort, and Victoria's beloved husband, died of typhoid fever in 1861. He was only 42 years old. The Queen was devastated. She remained in deep seclusion, and shunned her public duties for so many years that the people grew critical of her unrelenting sorrow. After the death of her husband, the joy of living deserted Victoria, and her life fell into an unswerving routine: following the rhythm of the seasons, she would call on the services of the GWR, LNWR and the London & South Western Railway (LSWR) to take her from Windsor to Balmoral, from Balmoral to Osborne, and from there back to Windsor in a sad triangle of journeys. The world went by, but the Queen remained the same. In the darkest years of Victoria's depression, her daughters grew closer to their mother, and lent her their strength and support. Victoria's twice-yearly journeys to Scotland created an odd, but touching new custom, for, if she wished to show her especial favour to a member of her family, she would share her sleeping saloon with those she wished to honour. The first person to be singled out in this way was her daughter Princess Helena. After Helena's marriage in 1866, her sisters Princess Louise and Princess Beatrice took her place, then Victoria's granddaughter, 'Moretta' (Princess Victoria of Prussia).

Left: GWR Diamond Jubilee train constructed in 1897, headed by engine no. 3041 *The Queen*. It pulls the Queen's saloon, two other royal saloons, a first class carriage and two brake vans. *GWR T7*

Opposite: Queen Victoria's day compartment in the LNWR saloon rebuilt in 1895 and on display at the NRM. The walls and ceiling are quilted in silk. Controls for electric lighting are set into the walls at the far end by the door, but oil and gas lamps were retained at Victoria's especial request. *NRM 115/79*

During Victoria's long reign, several railway companies were called upon to accommodate the Queen, but the two brightest stars in the firmament were undoubtedly the GWR and the LNWR. All the companies were eager to display their technical expertise to Victoria, who, unfortunately for them, was not as impressed by technological gadgetry as her husband. In 1868, Victoria had offered to pay the LNWR £800 to alter her existing carriage in order to remedy the problem of excessive heat. Instead, the company proposed to build two new vehicles, and to put the Queen's contribution towards this project. It was the only time in British history that a monarch actually paid for the cost of constructing a royal saloon. In 1869, the LNWR presented the Queen with a magnificent pair of six-wheeled saloons. The main compartment was lavishly upholstered, pelmeted and befrilled in blue and gold. An ornately patterned red carpet stretched from wall to wall, which afforded some insulation from the cold, for the only form of heating came in the shape of the old-fashioned footwarmers. These were not always sufficient for their purpose, for Neele records that on a journey from Ballater to Windsor in 1893, Princess Louise 'complained [that the] footwarmers were cold, a complaint not easily cured at this lonely place; an exchange however was made with some of the acetate of soda articles which met the case'[11].

Guards' compartment in the brake van of the GWR Diamond Jubilee Train, with cooking stoves and seats. *GWR CK2*

The Queen's equally elaborate toilet compartment was located at the other end of the room, and from there a main passageway led to the night saloon. The designers had included a flexible gangway between the two vehicles, but the Queen balked at the idea of stepping between two carriages at high speed, and insisted that the train be stopped before she moved between them. The idea of the gangway was in fact 20 years ahead of its time, for it would be another two decades before her subjects would enjoy this particular facility. In 1895, the LNWR deemed it time to bring the saloons up to date, but they also knew that Victoria would flatly refuse to accept any drastic changes. Undaunted, the company assigned its finest engineers to the problem. Victoria's rejection of their clever gangway must have rankled, for their solution was to join the two saloons together, and place them on a single underframe of 12 wheels. Victoria used this updated carriage until her death in 1901, and it now rests at the NRM, distinguished as being the only saloon used by Queen Victoria to survive intact to the present day.

As Victoria grew older, the intensity of her grief for Albert's death subsided slightly, and she began to show herself to her subjects again after so many years of seclusion. In turn, their criticism of her faded away, so that, in the last tranquil years of her life, Queen and subjects were in harmony again. The sixtieth year of Victoria's reign, 1897, dawned bright and glittering. The GWR produced its magnum opus in this year: the fabulous Diamond Jubilee

Train, and a new station at Windsor (now Windsor and Eton Station) for the Queen's especial use. Previously, the royal suite had been housed in a miscellaneous assortment of available carriages, but now, for the first time, there existed an entire, purpose-built Royal Train. Victoria, however, had grown accustomed to the furnishings of the GWR saloon of 1874 (built as a result of the changeover from broad- to standard-gauge track), and would not countenance any alteration. The solution of the GWR engineers, every bit as skilful as their LNWR counterparts, was to place the existing vehicle on a larger underframe and lengthen it at each end. It was decorated in fine green and white silks. The passenger saloons and the attendants' quarters repeated the green, cream and white colour scheme of the main compartment. The train was lit by electricity, with the notable exception of Victoria's saloon, where her favoured oil lamps were maintained, and the brake vans, which were lit by gas. Following the LNWR's example, flexible corridors, in the shape of bellows, were inserted between each of Victoria's carriages so that her attendants could wait on her, without having to clamber in and out of each carriage during stops every time the Queen desired their services.

The LNWR had got into serious trouble with the Queen for their experiments with electricity in her hallowed carriage. In June 1866, the electricians Martin and Varley had wired the LNWR train with a new 'electrical communication' system, which performed well.

Silver-plated cigarette case used in the 1897 Diamond Jubilee Royal Train. It comprises an ashtray, match striker, cigar cutter and cigarette box. *NRM CT970136*

Neele recalled that,

it was of course a novelty, and notices were posted up instructing passengers to "pull the handle" of the indicator, if necessary, to stop the train: one of the ladies-in-waiting begged me to have the notice covered up, she was sure if she travelled all day with those words staring in her face, she would be impelled to get up and pull the handle![12]

In 1868, inspired by their success, Martin and Varley designed an extra installation for the Queen's saloon, so that she could summon her dressers or pages by using an electric bell. At first, the invention seemed to do as it was bidden, but one morning at Perth, Princess Louise found that her dressers refused to answer her summons, and she was forced to dismount and call them herself.
An investigation into the matter showed that the entire system had failed, and, without further ado, the offending machinery was promptly dismantled, leaving Martin and Varley in disgrace.[13]

Queen Victoria's GWR Diamond Jubilee saloon, upholstered in French white silk, with green silk curtains, a green and white carpet, and fringes, tassels and laces also in green and white.
GWR CGC 14

Trials and tribulations: travelling with Queen Victoria

After Albert's early death in 1861, Victoria's formidably abrupt Highland servant, John Brown, became a close confidant of the Queen, but one who was thoroughly loathed by the rest of the Royal Household. On 14 May 1872, Neele recorded that, as they were passing Wigan, he encountered Brown in the train corridor. Brown had a way of paraphrasing the Queen's feelings into his own less-regal language, for when Neele enquired if everything was well, he was answered with, 'No! The Queen says the carriage is shaking like the devil.' At Perth, it was found that oil lamps had been leaking. Neele expressed the general feeling when he wrote that, 'John Brown's coarse phonograph had transmuted Her Majesty's gentle complaint!'[14]

Brown died in 1883, and soon afterwards Victoria's favour fell on one of her Indian servants, the Munshi Abdul Karim. He was never as unpopular as Brown with Neele and his colleagues, but Indian customs did baffle them for a while. By 1893, Neele could meet the Munshi's requests more easily for he wrote that,

carriage accommodation for the journeys to Scotland of the female contingent of the Queen's Munshi [had been requested], it being obligatory that the women should not be seen by the vulgar eye. At first I suspected that a whole harem had to be accommodated, but it came out in conversation that there was only one wife and daughter . . . [Neele assured the Palace that] a carriage should be sent which would meet all their requirements.[15]

In those that served her, the Queen inspired great devotion and loyalty, probably because she took such a personal interest in their lives. On 21 June 1895, on his 112th and final journey before retirement, the Queen summoned Neele to her saloon at Ballater. 'Looking at me with her full blue eyes', he wrote, 'she said she was sorry to hear that this was the last time I should accompany the train.'[16] She presented him with a framed engraving of the Royal Family (which he asked her to inscribe with a personal message) and, later, a large silver tray, engraved with her name.

Victoria's advancing age and the weight of her bereavement served to make the once delightful experience of rail travel a trial to her. Describing the heat of the night on 6 June 1887, Victoria recorded that,

Silver kettle used in Victoria's LNWR saloon by her personal attendant to make tea for the Queen. *BTF 9651*

Handle set into the wall of the attendants' compartment in Queen Victoria's LNWR saloon, to be pulled should the Queen wish to stop the train. *NRM T937418*

23

We had both windows open & I had as little on, almost as at home & only a thin cover—& yet we were stifled! The ice had melted [in the pails placed beneath the bed to cool the room] & had to be baled out, I c[oul]d. not sleep—till 1/2 p[ast].4—when there was some air—& I fell asleep soundly. Moretta was as still as anyone could be and never moved.[17]

The Royal Household also suffered its share of trials when obliged to travel with the Queen, although many difficulties sprung from Victoria's own entrenched prejudices and preferences. Putting the Queen to bed was one such problem. Her attendants and family would be kept busy fetching shawls, arranging cushions and bringing drinks until she was settled for the night. If every thought was given to the Queen's comfort while she travelled, the great ladies who attended her did not do quite so well. Before the introduction of connecting gangways, if the Queen required someone to attend her, it was necessary to stop the train so that the lady could descend from her carriage and enter the Queen's saloon. Too often, this would occur in the lonely wilds of Beattock Summit where no station existed. As the Queen's saloon was the only one on the train to be accompanied by a pair of folding steps, her lady-in-waiting would have to manage her skirts, and maintain her dignity, as she negotiated a flimsy footboard down to the ground. To regain their carriages presented another difficulty to the attendant ladies. Christopher Johnstone, the Caledonian manager, recounted his experience of 'pushing up' Lady Augusta Bruce into her carriage.[18]

Attendant's compartment adjoining Victoria's LNWR day saloon, equipped with basin and tea-making apparatus. It was used by the Queen's favoured servants, John Brown, and, after his death, by the Munshi Abdul Karim.
NRM T937399

Victoria refused to dine while travelling on her train, except on rare occasions. In this she was soon alone, for by 1877 Pullman dining cars were in regular service. Ordinary passengers would happily dine at high speed, but the Queen, frozen in time, insisted on dismounting and taking her meals in a station waiting room.

The GWR royal waiting room at Windsor Station, built to commemorate Queen Victoria's Diamond Jubilee, 1897. The clock on the mantelpiece is now on display at the NRM. *BTC 848/51*

Often, the waiting rooms would be ordinary chambers especially reserved for the royal meal, and accorded a few more comforts. But the stations that she visited regularly, such as Ballater or Paddington, had royal waiting rooms especially built for her use, and as lavishly decorated as her saloons. Breakfast was usually a race for her entourage, since the Queen ate little and would soon signal that the meal was over, forcing everybody to stop.

As well as her views on the unreliability of gadgetry, Victoria had decided and unalterable views on the speed her train should travel. Albert's comment of, 'Not so fast next time please, Mr Conductor' on alighting at Paddington after her first train ride in 1842, was possibly provoked by Victoria's reactions as they travelled, since he himself was no stranger to the experience. Thereafter, Victoria's Royal Train was never permitted to exceed 40 mph during daylight, and 30 mph at night. Both the GWR and the LNWR thoughtfully grafted a signal system into the design of the saloon, so that her household could slow the train if the Queen wished. In reality, the speed limits the Queen imposed were often exceeded, but she was unaware of this if all went smoothly and quietly.

The officials in charge of the Royal Train sometimes went to great lengths in order to protect the Queen from learning of the dangers which accompanied rail travel. On 1 June 1898, Victoria was journeying south after a visit to Balmoral. Five miles south of Aberdeen, just

Pendulum clock once displayed on the mantelpiece in the royal waiting room at Windsor Station, c1850. *NRM CT970132*

past Cove Bay, driver David Fenwick climbed onto the tender, piled high with coal, to adjust the communication cord, and struck his head on the overbridge. The fireman looked around, saw that he had vanished, and in panic began to sound the whistle to alert the officials that something terrible had occurred. To stop the train, and so disquiet the Queen, was out of the question, and the official in charge of the journey, Tom Macdonald, had to scramble over the tender and drop down into the cab. In the meantime, Cove Bay had signalled Perth Station, where the train was due to stop, that half a human head in a driver's cap had been found on the line. The Royal Train would glide into Perth bedecked with a mutilated human body on its tender. In the event, only a few senior officials were told of the accident. The engines were speedily uncoupled and taken out of public sight. The Queen was informed gently of the mishap, and reacted characteristically by sending a personal wreath to the funeral three days later.

Victoria may have been safer than the ordinary passenger when she travelled by train, but she was still vulnerable to the assassin who haunts every head of state. On 2 March 1882, she wrote in her journal:

Just as we were driving off from the station [Windsor], the people or rather the Eton boys, cheered, and at the same time there was the sound of what I thought was an explosion from the engine . . . I then realised that it was a shot, which must have been meant for me . . .. Great excitement prevails. Nothing can exceed dearest Beatrice's courage and calmness, for she saw . . . the man take aim and fire straight into the carriage, but she never said a word, observing that I was not frightened.[19]

Roderick Maclean, the would-be assassin, was later judged to be insane and was incarcerated in an asylum.

Letter sent to each of the main railway companies by Victoria's equerry, dated 26 August 1852. In it he relays the Queen's annoyance at recent infringements of the speed limit she imposes on the Royal Train and her wish that it be strictly observed in the future. He remarks pointedly, 'This order has probably arisen from one of the Directors [of a railway company] telling Her Majesty last year that they had been driving the Train at the rate of 60 miles an hour, a gratuitous piece of information which very naturally alarmed Her Majesty, although it was probably incorrect.' *GWR B 9517a/GWR B 9517b*

The final journey

The Queen survived the threat of violent death to pass away peacefully, an old lady, at her beloved Osborne House on 22 January 1901. In life, her train journeys had run more or less like clockwork, but in death, Victoria's final journey by rail was beset by the inefficiency which had so roused her to fury. King Edward VII had decreed that his mother should be taken to London by the London, Brighton & South Coast Railway (LB&SCR). Victoria's treasured Diamond Jubilee saloon was enlisted for the last time, to take her on to Windsor. The interior was slightly altered to make room for the coffin, and the saloon itself attached to a motley collection of hearse carriages. The delays (beginning at Gosport, where the mourners were unable to find their allotted places on the train) were resolved by the driver of the train, who drove it at a speed of 80 mph, twice what Victoria had allowed while she lived. Consequently, the train arrived at Victoria Station two minutes early. Her coffin was placed on a gun carriage, then solemnly drawn through the streets of London to Paddington, watched by the same curious eyes which had scrutinised the Queen so closely in life. The GWR saloon had been uncoupled and was waiting at the station, now reunited with the remainder of the Diamond Jubilee Train. Bewreathed and festooned with purple and white decorations, this was truly a Royal Train. Headed by an engine temporarily named the *Royal Sovereign*, each carriage was full of European crowned heads who had come to mark Victoria's death.

The grave of David Fenwick, the driver who was accidentally decapitated during a Royal Train journey. The headstone reads 'Erected by Queen Victoria as a mark of sympathy in memory of David Fenwick engine driver aged 52 years who was fatally injured when driving the Royal Train from Aberdeen to Perth on 21 June 1898.' *SRX 474*

The funeral train had been booked to leave at 1.32 p.m. for Windsor, but ran eight minutes late. There were more problems when it arrived at Windsor, for the horses had become restive during the wait in the icy cold, and could not be used to pull the coffin. The hawsers attached to the gun carriage had also frozen, but a quick-thinking naval officer ordered that communication cords be cut from the passenger coaches and attached to the gun carriage. Sailors were pressed into service to pull it to St George's Chapel at Windsor Castle, where the funeral finally took place.

The railways had brought Albert and Victoria together in courtship more than 60 years earlier, and now they brought Victoria home to rest beside him. She had encouraged the railways as they took their first steps into a world that was uncertain how to receive them, she had given them credibility, and if they had outpaced her, they had grown strong because of her belief in them, a fact which they never forgot. The GWR's Diamond Jubilee ode had ended with the fitting accolade:

Hark! cannon, clarion, drums;
Bells peal; Victoria comes
Benign, serene!
Now who shall dare gainsay
Railwaymen place to-day,
While all thy people pray
"God Save the Queen!"[20]

GWR *Royal Sovereign*, which pulled Queen Victoria's funeral train from London to Windsor on 2 February 1901. The engine is decorated with a wreath of white immortelles and the Royal Arms framed by purple drapes. *BTC 2266/58*

KING EDWARD VII
and the golden age of Royal Train travel

The Royal Train in fashion

The new King was destined to rule for only nine years. Edward, Prince of Wales, was a grandfather aged 60 when Victoria died, having lived his life in the awe-inspiring shadow of his legendary mother. In 1863, Victoria had selected Princess Alexandra of Denmark, known as 'Alix', as a bride for Edward ('Bertie'), in the hope that a strong and loving wife would exert a guiding influence over his weak nature. Alexandra completely frustrated the Queen's hopes, for the 'Marlborough House set', as the Prince and Princess's fashionable circle was known, lived at the very centre of high society.

The railways had offered the pleasure-seeking Prince an ideal way to travel from one amusement to another. One of Edward's most favoured locations was Brighton, and the LB&SCR was his company of choice. A six-wheel saloon was built for him, with two main compartments and a smoking room, which he used until the Diamond Jubilee year of 1897, when a magnificent Royal Train was fashioned for his family's use. It was as opulently furnished as the carriages provided for Queen Victoria, but in the style that Edward was to encourage when he became King. The Prince's compartment had a gentlemen's club atmosphere about it, being upholstered in dark green morocco leather and crimson carpeting, while Alexandra's quarters were finished in velvet with a soft grey–green carpet, and panelled with inlaid woods. In some ways the train surpassed Victoria's conveyances for it was lit by electricity, and new electric heaters proudly resided in the two royal compartments.

Prince Albert had made arrangements for the purchase of a Norfolk estate, Sandringham House, so that his son would have a country residence. Together, the Prince and Princess of Wales turned Sandringham into a warm and friendly home, into which their guests were welcomed with a merry informality. The Great Eastern Railway (GER), whose network covered Norfolk, saw which way the wind was likely to blow for many years to come, and busied itself in producing a fabulous Royal Train for the entire family. The first saloon was built in 1897 for the Prince of Wales, and the following year a saloon for Alexandra was added, both carriages remaining in use until the accession in 1901. To commemorate this event, the GER built a 50-foot-long carriage which contained a saloon each for the King and Queen. The carriages were lit by gas, but served with electric bell pushes and a steam heating system.

The nearest station to Sandringham was Wolferton. It was a small wayside station on the Lynn & Hunstanton branch line out in the windblown wilds of rural Norfolk, and very different to the palatial London stations from which a royal party would begin its journey. Edward himself paid to have improvements

Opposite: King Edward (far left, in feathered hat) and Queen Alexandra (on his left) dismount at Newcastle upon Tyne Station, September 1906. *NRM 90/80*

made to the tiny station, and is said to have used the royal waiting room for entertaining his numerous guests during the shooting season. Although Sandringham was a favourite of George V and George VI in later years, Wolferton station was at its zenith in Edwardian days, when its oak-panelled portals were graced by Kaiser Wilhelm II of Germany, Tsar Nicholas II of Russia, and prominent politicians of the day. Hordes of aristocratic travellers would arrive at the station on their way to Sandringham as house guests of the King.

All change

Once Edward became King, the sun of royal favour ceased to shine on Balmoral and Osborne, taking with it the coveted patronage enjoyed by the railway companies which served them. Osborne House was donated to the nation, and Balmoral was accorded only one visit a year. However, Edward and Alexandra did not ignore Scotland entirely, for they used the royal saloon built for them by the little Great North of Scotland Railway (GNSR) for

Right: White silk timetable produced by the SER for the use of the Prince of Wales and Princess Alexandra of Denmark on their journey from Gravesend to Bricklayers Arms, 7 March 1863. Such opulent timetables were often used during the long history of the Royal Train. *NRM CT970130*

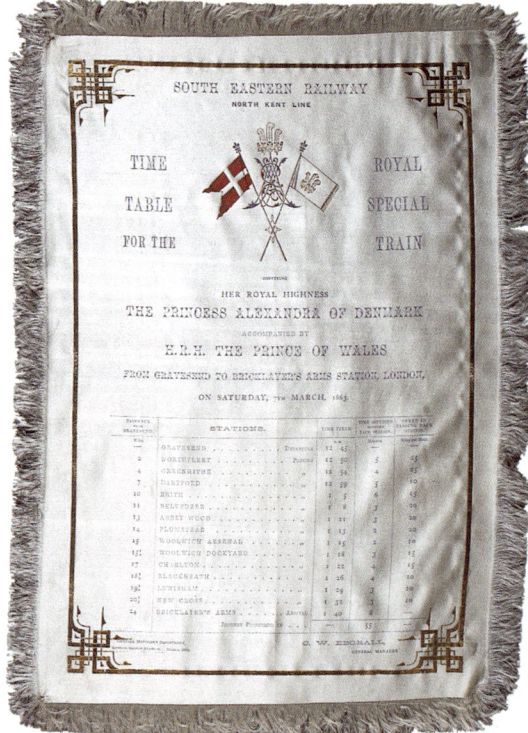

Far right: The Prince of Wales leaves Great Yarmouth Southtown Station in June 1872, via the triumphal arch raised for the occasion. *447/97*

excursions from Balmoral. Windsor Castle was not forsaken by Edward either. On 28 October 1901, soon after his accession, Edward visited Windsor Station, where he expressed the opinion that the royal waiting room was very small for his needs, since he anticipated a far heavier use of the facility than before. He requested that improvements be completed by the following year. Anxious to please, the GWR rushed to fulfil the request. Since it had been built for Queen Victoria, the accommodation of the existing waiting room had been designed to

shelter the ladies of the Royal Household. The company now extended it to include a gentlemen's salon with conveniences, spending a total of £67,588 0s 5d (over £3 million at today's prices) on the renovations.

The year 1902 heralded the beginning of a boom era for Royal Train construction. The South Eastern & Chatham Railway (SE&CR) assembled a train for use in the southern regions of England. It was very popular with the Royal Family and was used until the outbreak

Smoking room in the King's day compartment of the LNWR Royal Train. Its leather and wood opulence and the drinks decanters lend it the ambience of an Edwardian gentlemen's club. *NRM T937373*

of the Second World War. However, it was the LNWR who again won most royal favour. They chose to celebrate the accession by constructing a new Royal Train for the monarch, which was the last word in up-to-date technology. Edward had sampled something like it in 1902, when he and Alexandra used the Duke of Sutherland's private saloon to travel from Invergordon to Ballater. The Duke had commissioned the LNWR to construct this carriage for him in 1899, and it is now on display at the NRM. The company incorporated several key elements of the Duke's saloon into the design of the new carriages, which were distinguished by being the largest royal saloons yet built. It is said that Edward asked for his quarters to be decorated in a nautical style. Certainly the white, enamelled style does suggest the interior of a yacht, but the saloon is also fitted with ingenious gadgets, such as electric cigar lighters. Alexandra's saloon was as feminine in decor as the King's was masculine. The plump

The King's saloon built for Edward VII by the Great Eastern Railway in 1903. The walls and seats were lined in morocco leather dyed in the company blue, as were the carpets and curtains. *SX 469*

indulgences of Victoria's saloon were forsaken in favour of more elegant flowing lines. The new Queen's bedroom was fitted with two beds, one for herself and one for her second daughter, Princess Victoria, who was her constant companion. Alexandra's own bed was distinguished by the exotic silken tent hung over it, which she felt would protect her from draughts, but its inclusion may have been the product of her romantic fascination with the Orient. The saloon included two dressing rooms, one for the Queen and one for the Princess. Both saloons were later adapted to the tastes of King George V and Queen Mary, and are displayed at the NRM.

The LNWR also incorporated one other feature which Queen Victoria never permitted in her Royal Train: two dining cars, one for the use of the royal travellers, and the other for their entourage. This innovation allowed journey times to be shortened dramatically, for there was no need for the tedious stops for meals at station hotels or waiting rooms upon which Victoria had insisted. The royal dining car, built by the LNWR but part of the West Coast Joint Stock stable owned jointly by the LNWR and Caledonian Railway, was used until 1956, and can be viewed at the NRM.

The third Royal Train built for Edward was completed some years later in 1908–09 by two of the three East Coast Joint Stock (ECJS) partners, the Great Northern Railway and the North Eastern Railway. It comprised two massive 12-wheel saloons for the King and Queen, which were fitted out for day and night use. Both were decorated in the style of Louis XVI, and a discreet innovation was the inclusion of hidden tubular lights and pressure ventilation. Refurbished later for King George V and Queen Mary, both saloons form part of the National Collection.

Gadgets installed in King Edward's saloon in the LNWR Royal Train. *NRM 94/97*

King's day compartment in the LNWR Royal Train, built in 1902. The saloon is finished in nautical white enamel and equipped with electric lighting and a ventilation fan. *BTC 312/66*

Royal Victorian Medal, made of gold, presented to Royal Train Driver D Hughes by Edward VII on 29 July 1901. The medal shows a bust of Queen Victoria, and is awarded in recognition of personal service to the monarch. Stanley Butler, Royal Train Foreman 1967–93, was awarded the silver version of the medal in 1989. *NRM CT970138*

Postcard showing Queen Alexandra's bedroom in the LNWR Royal Train, most notable for the tent over the bed which the Queen felt would keep out drafts. The second bed, in the foreground, was used by Alexandra's daughter, Princess Louise. *NRM 1706/85*

Mishaps, pranks and danger

Although Edward believed that the railway companies should try new ideas, he was no less exacting than his mother in the standards he expected the Royal Train to meet. G P Neele's reminiscences for 19 July 1890 relate one occasion on which he was summoned to the then Prince's saloon:

and there, with not unreasonable annoyance, he called my attention to the state of the table in the saloon. It was covered with fine black dust, which, he said, had not only come down on himself and his table, but had also descended on the dresses of the ladies accompanying the party. What could be done? What could be said? Unfortunately the cause was too apparent—all this grit and dust had come through some new fangled roof ventilators the carriage department had fitted into the compartment. Those ventilators never worked again so long as His Royal Highness used that vehicle![1]

However, His Royal Highness was also capable of the same thoughtfulness and courtesy as Victoria, in showing his appreciation of the efforts made by the staff of the train. Five years earlier, in April 1885, after a trip to Ireland, he had summoned Neele to Marlborough House. Neele had been harbouring a rather guilty conscience:

I could glean no tidings as to the reason of my attendance being required, and my fears warned me that there might be some enquiry as to the hot axle and the fast running; however I left with a light heart and a very pleasant memory, for after a kind reception, His Royal

Highness presented me with a gold pencil case, ornamented with the Prince's feathers, as a memento of his sense of attention to him on this Irish journey.[2]

Nevertheless, not all staff members could possibly expect as much. In 1909, near the end of their reign, the King and Queen travelled to Germany to meet their relation, Kaiser Wilhelm II. At dinner, served on the train, a footman bent to serve Alexandra from a plate of quails,

the train gave a lurch and the plate landed on the Queen, leaving one unfortunate bird hanging from her toupée (she was bald by this time). She took the incident in characteristic good humour, which was as well, for a waiter upset a carafe of claret over the table later that same meal.

Many years earlier, another, more serious mishap had befallen the Prince and his family on 11 May 1875, as they travelled from London to Windsor to meet with Victoria before she

Footman's compartment in the LNWR Royal Train, adjacent to the King's saloon. A comfortable green leather chair sits beside a bank of electrical machinery. The footman was also provided with tea-making facilities. *NRM T939388*

departed for Balmoral. As the saloon rolled over the viaduct near Eton Wick, a schoolboy took careful aim with his catapult and fired a stone at the window. It smashed through the quarter-inch-thick pane, and showered the startled royals with splinters of glass. Maintaining a regal composure, they refrained from alerting the GWR policemen who were travelling on the train, until they reached Windsor, whereupon the Prince dismounted, holding a piece of glass in his hand, and commented that one of the schoolboys must have been playing with a ball. The next day, Queen Victoria herself sent a message to the station asking if the culprit had been identified, only to learn that two boys had admitted throwing stones at the train, but not at that precise spot.

West Coast Joint Stock dining car No. 76. After winning a prize at the Paris Exhibition in 1900 it was attached to Edward VII's LNWR Royal Train and served under three kings before being withdrawn from service in 1956. *NRM CT970145*

The SER saloon as used by Edward and Alexandra in Brussels in 1900, when an attempt was made on their lives. The would-be assassin's bullet lodged above the right-hand-side window, having been fired through the open window opposite. *BTC 318/66*

Edward, like his mother before him, escaped the assassin's bullet, and died peacefully at Buckingham Palace on 6 May 1910. The country ground to a halt as his subjects mourned the passing of a popular king. On Friday 20 May, Windsor Station closed its doors to the public and prepared to receive the remains of another dead monarch. Edward's funeral bore some odd resemblances to that of his mother nine years before. As his coffin arrived at Paddington Station, a

The incident appears to have been motivated by nothing more than mischief, but the Royal Family was destined to be the object of altogether more serious intentions in 1900. On a visit to Alexandra's home in Copenhagen, the royal party had arrived at Brussels Station on 4 April, where Sipido, a 15-year-old anarchist, was lying in wait for them. Edward recorded his impressions of the next few chaotic moments in a telegram to Alice Keppel: 'As we were leaving Brussels a man jumped on the step of our carriage and fired a pistol at us through the open window. I don't think there was a bullet in it.'[3] There was; in fact, there were five more. The bullet passed between the heads of the Prince and Princess, but the only member of the party to lose composure was Alexandra's Chinese dog. The stationmaster seized Sipido, disarmed him and dragged him away.

Queen Victoria's Diamond Jubilee saloon, as converted for the funeral journey of Edward VII. The furniture has been removed to allow room for the catafalque, where the coffin rested, and the walls are draped in purple and white. *GWR CGC 18*

photographer who had climbed up onto the glass roof put his foot through a pane and showered the spectators below with splinters: a similar incident had occurred during Victoria's funeral. The GWR Royal Train left London just before noon, headed by the *King Edward* engine. On arrival at Windsor, the memory of the near-fiasco with the horses still being sharp, the King's coffin on its gun carriage was efficiently pulled to St George's Chapel by sailors who were ready and waiting,

perhaps a fitting tribute to Edward's keen nautical interests.

The future seemed bright and untroubled when Edward's son, George V, took the throne, but just a few years after his accession the world exploded into war. It became the Royal Family's role to travel the country, giving the nation much-needed moral support, and to accomplish this the new King assigned a very special role to the Royal Train.

Funeral cortège of Edward VII outside Windsor Station, 20 May 1910. Grenadier Guards flank the convoy of sailors enlisted to pull the gun carriage holding Edward's coffin to St George's Chapel at Windsor Castle. *BTC 813/51*

KING GEORGE V
a new role for the Royal Train

The lazy, golden years of the Royal Train ended with the death of Edward VII. The days when railway companies had the leisure to plan and construct new ways of conveying the monarch in gilded splendour were over. The threat of war rumbled in the distance.

The new King and Queen, George and Mary (or 'May', as the family called her) inherited five British Royal Trains. The first and foremost was the well-established LNWR train which was to lead the way in the changes the King was to make to royal travel. Second was the ECJS train, used for journeys between London and Sandringham. In 1925 it was converted to day use when the former King's saloon was refurbished to accommodate Queen Mary and the former Queen's saloon was upgraded to accommodate both George and Mary, becoming known as 'Their Majesties' Saloon'. This latter saloon was never well-liked by them and was eventually phased out of royal service.

Left: Day compartment of the East Coast Joint Stock Queen's saloon, on display at the NRM. Originally constructed for Edward VII in 1908, it was converted for Queen Mary in 1925. Queen Elizabeth, later the Queen Mother, used it, after further adaptation, until 1977. *NRM T939378*

Opposite: The King (second from left) tries his hand at driving GWR No. 4082 *Windsor Castle* on a visit to Swindon Works on 28 April 1924. Beside him are Queen Mary, the Chairman of the GWR, the General Manager and the Chief Mechanical Engineer. *NRM 1156/85*

King George V (obscured) and Queen Mary (centre, in white) dismount from the Royal Train at Ashton, during a tour of the industrial areas of Lancashire in 1913. With war a possibility, the King and Queen were anxious to show support for those involved in vital industries. *HOR F 1944*

Both ECJS saloons are part of the National Collection, and the Queen's saloon is on display in the NRM. Third and fourth were the SE&CR and LB&SCR trains, which belonged to the golden Edwardian days, and although they remained part of the royal fleet they were also withdrawn from service in the 1930s. The only addition to the collection of royal vehicles was a royal saloon provided by the Midland Railway in 1912, but it was seldom used, and both it and the old GER Royal Train were withdrawn from service when the railway map of England was redrawn in 1923. In this year the 'Big Four' railway companies came into existence: the London, Midland & Scottish (LMS), the London & North Eastern Railway (LNER), the GWR and the Southern Railway (SR).

Like his father, George encouraged the staff members of the Royal Train to push the boundaries of its achievements further, although this could have its drawbacks. His diary entry

King George V and Queen Mary walk towards the waiting Royal Train after opening the King George Dock at Hull on 26 June 1914. *NRM 92/97*

for 14 July 1903, when he was still Prince of Wales, reads:

May and I left Paddington with Lady Mary for Cornwall by the Great Western. We made a splendid run to Plymouth without stopping doing the 246 miles in 3 hrs. 53 3/4 mins. which is the world's record, breaking all previous records. It is interesting no doubt to have done it; but it was a very disagreeable journey & we shook about a great deal & I couldn't sleep at all.[1]

The declaration of war in 1914 changed the role of the Royal Train forever. The King and Queen believed that they could make a valuable contribution to boost the morale of the country during the years that were to follow. Their plan was to tour the country as often as possible, in order to inspect troops, factories and hospitals. Where convenient, the motor car was employed, but the Royal Train was accorded a vital place in the King's war strategy. He recognised that they could no longer rely on the hospitality of the aristocracy over long periods, because even

the nobility would be suffering under the shortages of food and other necessities. The King himself closed Balmoral for the duration of the war, and the Royal Train, now a working palace on wheels, took on the role of a mobile court, and a home for the Royal Family while they were on tour. Just as the railways were commandeered by the government for the vital work of troop and supply transportation, the LNWR Royal Train was enlisted for war service by the King. He ordered the dressing rooms in each saloon to be fitted with copper and silver-plated bathtubs, which would enable the Royal Family to remain on board the train for extended periods. The accommodation for the Royal Household also had bathing facilities added, and was refurbished in a more functional style. Mary, whose serious and reserved character had been overshadowed by her flamboyant mother-in-law, Queen Alexandra, marked her emancipation by having the fanciful oriental tent removed from over her

The Queen's bedroom in the LNWR Royal Train on display at the NRM. Inheriting it from Queen Alexandra, Queen Mary had the tent over the bed removed and the room redecorated. *NRM CT970147*

The King's bedroom in the LNWR train after the refurbishments by Queen Mary. The far wall is studded with controls, and the room is equipped with electric lights and fans. *NRM T937374*

The LNWR Royal Train curves gracefully around the landscape between Dolphinton Junction and Carnwath in Scotland, c1919. *BTC 441/53*

bed. These changes can be seen in the displayed carriages at the NRM.

It was perhaps appropriate that one of the first to hear the news of the war's end was a key member of the Royal Train staff, Samuel Maun, stationmaster at Windsor. On 11 November 1918, George's niece, Princess Alice, confided that an armistice had been signed in a railway carriage near Paris at 6.00 a.m. that morning, but swore him to secrecy until the official announcement was made at 11.00 a.m.

After the war, George retained his keen interest in the railways. On 28 April 1924, he and Queen Mary visited the GWR Works at Swindon, when he was invited to take the controls of the new and aptly named *Windsor Castle* locomotive. In 1927, he was pleased to give his permission to the GWR to name a new engine the *King George V*. Despite this show of affinity and affection, the Royal Family had been discovering the advantages offered them by a new form of locomotion: the motor car. The Royal Family were able to revisit their holiday home at Balmoral in 1919, but the railway strike which coincided with this event ended any thoughts of returning from there by train. In earlier decades, the strike would have been a serious inconvenience, but the King was

The LNWR King's saloon on display at the NRM. Designed for use by Edward VII in 1902, it was also used by George V and George VI. *NRM CT970148*

able to turn to the motor car for help, and made the journey home by road. In 1925, he discussed the issue with Maun, who reports that the King said,

"When I first came here I had to drive to Paddington, train to Windsor, and drove to the Castle. Now I get in my car at the front door and am at Buckingham Palace in 45 minutes. Don't you think it is more convenient?" I replied, "Yes, sir, although I am a railway man it does seem so."[2]

The GWR train, once used frequently to take the Royal Family from London to Windsor, was withdrawn from service in 1928, possibly a

casualty of the motor car's increasing popularity with the King.

'Georgie and May' reigned for 25 years, celebrating their Silver Jubilee in 1935. However, in the overcast, January gloom of 1936 George's weak health declined, and he died at Sandringham. The LNER's first-class saloon, which had conveyed Queen Alexandra's body from Sandringham to London on her death 11 years earlier, was speedily despatched to Stratford Works for the necessary alterations for its conversion to a royal hearse carriage. In 24 hours, all its internal fittings had been removed, the walls were lined with black and

mauve velvet, the windows were painted black, the lighting subdued and a catafalque, or bier, was placed in readiness for the coffin. The King lay in state at Westminster, before being slowly carried in a mile-long cortège on the traditional gun carriage through the crowded London streets. The entrance to Paddington Station was covered in heavy, royal-purple draperies, with wreaths of laurels and Flanders poppies positioned along the platform. Since the old GWR train no longer existed, the LNER train was enlisted for the journey. Appropriately, the engine selected to take the King to his final resting place was his old friend, *Windsor Castle*.

Cover of the programme of train arrangements produced by the Lancashire & Yorkshire Railway and the LNWR for the royal tour of 1913. Such booklets detailed the massive arrangements required by the railway system to enable the Royal Train to pass over lines belonging to several different companies without undue disruption to normal traffic. *NRM CT970131*

The LNWR Queen's day saloon on display at the NRM. The green colour scheme complements that of the King's day compartment, but has been somewhat softened by the addition of tasselled and pelmeted brocade curtains around the room. *NRM CT970146*

KING GEORGE VI AND PRINCESS ELIZABETH
the Royal Train in war and peace

The close acquaintance of King George VI ('Bertie') with the Royal Train began when he was still the Duke of York. Bertie's older brother, David, Prince of Wales, became increasingly involved with his American mistress, Mrs Simpson, to the detriment of his public duties. The Duke and Duchess of York, who held that duty came before personal considerations, increased their share of engagements to fill the gap, travelling frequently on the Royal Train.

The shy Duke and his vivacious Duchess, Elizabeth, with their children, Elizabeth and Margaret Rose, and their governess, Marion Crawford ('Crawfie'), had lived quietly in a London townhouse. The death of George V, and the subsequent abdication of the Duke's brother David (Edward VIII) in December 1936, dramatically changed the relatively sedate lives of the small family. Now King and Queen, the demands on George and Elizabeth's time and energy increased, whilst the time they had been accustomed to spending with their daughters diminished. Their annual August holiday, for example, beginning with an overnight railway journey up to Ballater in Scotland aboard the old family favourite, the Edwardian LNWR train, suddenly became more precious.

Public duties obliged the new King and Queen to leave their children for state visits abroad. In 1939, George and Elizabeth made a seven-week tour of America and Canada. Twenty-four coaches were assembled for the royal party, divided into two trains: a Royal Train which was intended to act as their home for the duration of the tour; and a Pilot Train to house reporters, police and technicians, and which would travel 30 minutes ahead of the Royal Train.

The Canadian Royal Train surpassed its British cousins: it was fitted out with the latest technology, being air-conditioned and containing radio sets and telephones. The train was designed to be as self-sufficient as possible: even milk consumed aboard the train was specially pasteurised and labelled 'Royal Train'. There was also a barber's shop and post office. Such was the glamour surrounding the Royal Train that this last proved to be very popular with the local people, who would gather wherever it stopped so that the letters they

posted would bear the Royal Train stamp. It was estimated that in one day some 250,000 letters would pass through the office. The route of the North American trip stretched from Quebec to Vancouver, thundered over Mount Robson in the Rockies at nearly 13,000 feet, and over the border into America. The train carried the King and Queen to official engagements in Washington and New York, and thence back into Canada from where they finally set sail for home.

The war effort

It would be six years before the Royal Family would travel anywhere abroad again, for war tore Europe apart for the second time in 25 years, just months after their return from Canada. Balmoral was again covered in dustsheets until such time as it was safe to return. The King and Queen took the same view as George's parents, that the role of the monarchy in wartime was to be visible in the

The King's bathroom in the LNWR Royal Train on display in the NRM. It was fitted with a new ceramic bath and washbasin in August 1941. A small red line was painted just above the plughole, probably to indicate the maximum depth at which water would not spill from the bath whilst the train was in motion, and perhaps also the level of water permitted in baths during wartime shortages. *NRM C797002*

support of its people, and that the role of the Royal Train was to support this aim. The days of the LNWR train were coming to a close. Its old, pre-1923 colours made it an easy target for enemy action, so it was painted in the 'crimson lake' hue of its new owners, the LMS, to make it indistinguishable from other carriages belonging to the company. Following the precedent set by his father, King George VI again turned the train into a mobile court, and a home-away-from-home. Functional ceramic baths replaced the old, ornate, silver-plated tubs, and a short red line was painted five inches above the plughole, possibly a wartime economy measure.

Ever mindful of improvements which could be made to the royal vehicles, and unhappy with the low level of security afforded by the fragile wooden bodies of the saloons, the LMS had made the decision to construct an entirely new Royal Train in 1938. The restrictions imposed

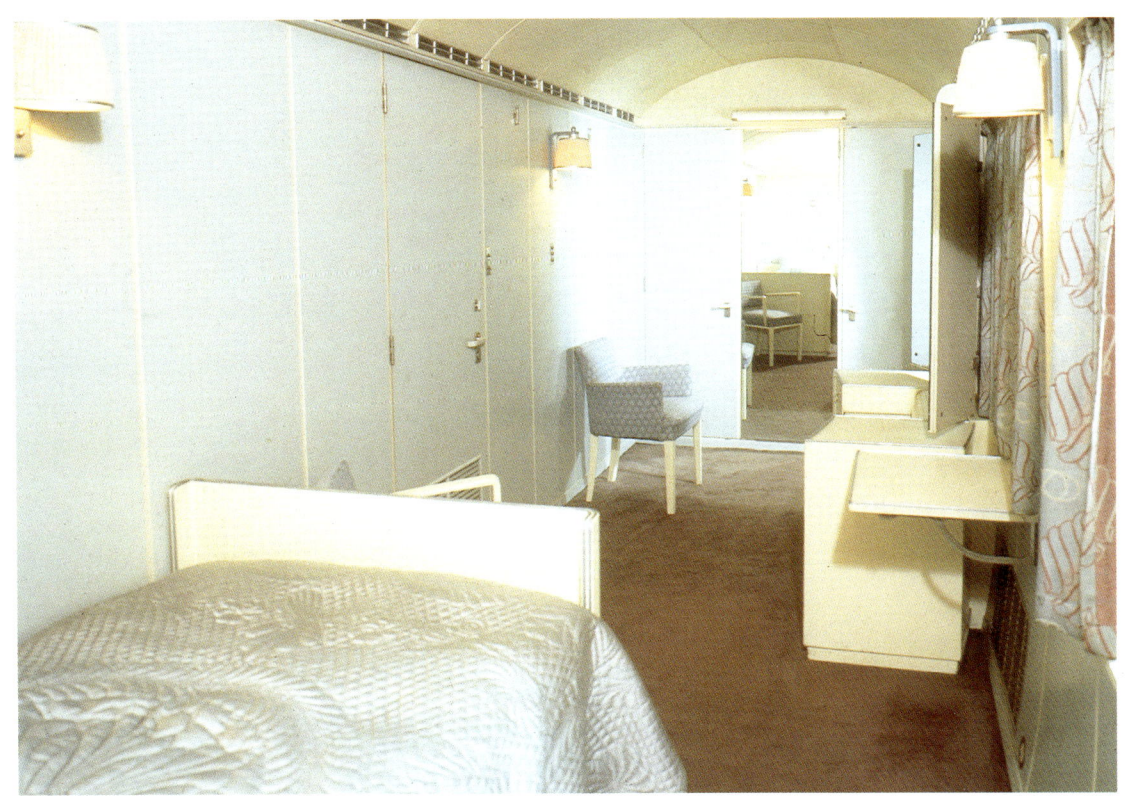

The Queen's bedroom in LMS saloon No. 799, built in 1941 and used by Queen Elizabeth II and her mother until 1977. It is on display at the NRM.
NRM T939373

by the war meant that in 1941 only three new vehicles were built, two royal saloons for the King and Queen (the latter is on display at the NRM), and a service car. Both saloons contained day and night accommodation, including bathrooms and flatlets for personal attendants. Discretion and functional efficiency were the keynotes which characterised the new regime. Nevertheless, the LMS diligently followed the tradition of fitting royal conveyances with the most up-to-date gadgetry, and the saloons bristled with modern technology. The windows were double-glazed to protect against drafts and intrusive noise, and

also fitted with dehydrators to prevent condensation. Ice was employed to provide air-conditioning, and a selection of six levels of temperature, linked to a thermostat, could be made via the advanced steam and electric heating systems. A private telephone system within the saloons was installed, as well as a 25-line telephone exchange for the entire train and buzzers with which to summon staff.

Unfortunately, despite the elaborate care taken by the LMS to provide every comfort, the kingly wrath would sometimes fall on the heads of its hapless staff. There is a story that, while

Queen's day compartment in the LMS wartime saloon. Its austere lines present a stark contrast to the opulent blue splendour of Queen Victoria's day saloon. *NRM T939372*

the Royal Train was stabled overnight at Aberlady Station during the war, the King's valet reported to the officials aboard the train that His Majesty's bath water would not drain away. On investigation, it was discovered that the track was curved and elevated on one side, so that the plughole was higher than the level of the water in the tub. Nothing could be done that evening, but the situation was worsened the following morning when an angry King complained that, since his bed was on the higher side of the incline, he had tended to fall out of bed during the night. The Queen had suffered a similar discomfort but had said nothing. Nonetheless, the conscientious officials took care to rest the coach on a straight piece of track the next night.

Both the existence of the new Royal Train and its subsequent movements were kept secret for security reasons. Two codewords, 'Grove' and 'Deepdene', were devised to denote the activities of the Royal Train during these years and for some time after. If the King was travelling, then 'Grove' signalled that the entire train was in use and could be identified by means of four headlamps or white disks arranged on the front of the engine. 'Deepdene' signified a train which was carrying royalty other than the King. Few people living in the areas visited by the King and Queen knew of their visit in advance. The press was silent about the movements of the Royal Family, but an examination of the logbooks kept as a record of the movements of the Royal Train show how active George and Elizabeth were during the war period, and the vast areas of the realm they covered. From 28 to 31 October 1941, they visited Leeds, Doncaster, Sheffield, Bolton Abbey, Blackburn, Leyland, Newton-le-Willows, Prescot and Garstang Town. The year 1942 was characterised by similar long journeys: for example, from 5 to 8 May, the Royal Train took them from Paddington to Penzance, Thurso, Falmouth, Liskeard, Plymouth, Totnes, Kingswear, Exeter and then to Windsor, presumably to visit their children. The same punishing schedule was followed in the remaining years of the war.

GWR Royal Train towel box, made from stained pine, in use between 1900 and 1940. *NRM CT970135*

A munitions worker at the LNER's Doncaster Works demonstrates machinery to Queen Elizabeth, October 1941. Such visits, made aboard the Royal Train, were part of the Royal Family's own morale-boosting contribution to the war effort. *DON 41/103*

Part of Queen Elizabeth's prized Minton 'Cheviot' dinner service, used aboard the 1940s GWR Royal Train. *NRM CT970133*

Other changes were taking place in the sheds and workshops of the railway companies. In 1940, the GWR also produced two new royal saloons, designed for daytime use only, which were employed mainly by Queen Mary and by chief government officials during the war. In 1945, two other coaches completed the GWR Royal Train and these offered both day and night accommodation, bathroom and catering facilities. These remained in use well into the next reign. Peace in 1945 signalled the all-change for the railway industry once more, and three years later, at the stroke of midnight on 1 January 1948, the privately-owned 'Big Four' railway companies were transformed into a government-run organisation split into six regions and dubbed 'British Railways'.

A change of track: the princess and the train

The end of the Second World War also marked the end of Princess Elizabeth's childhood. She and Lieutenant Philip Mountbatten, a member of the exiled Greek royal family, made their wish to marry known to her parents. A formal

Dining room in the GWR saloon No. 9006, built in the 1940s. The saloon has been loaned to the West Somerset Railway for display. *NRM 747/84*

announcement of the engagement was postponed until the Royal Family had completed a six-week tour of South Africa. They set sail for Africa on 21 February 1947, where a fabulous Royal Train, known as the 'White Train', was waiting for them. It measured a third of a mile long and its distinctive ivory and gold appearance reflected the sunlight. Captivated by the glamour and mystique of the beautiful train and its distinguished passengers, crowds would gather at each station to gaze at the train, or travel miles into the veld to watch it go by. Like the Canadian Royal Train, the White Train was a marvel of technology and the last word in comfort. It was air-conditioned throughout, with a thermostat to control the temperature in the saloons, whilst generators powered the up-to-date electric irons, kettles, refrigerators, vacuum cleaners, radio-gramophone and public-address system. The train also contained

a post office and a telephone exchange which was connected to the main exchange when the train was at rest.

On the royal party's return, the engagement of Elizabeth and Philip was declared on 10 July. They were married at Westminster Abbey on 20 November 1947. It was the SR which was again enlisted to provide the honeymoon train as it had for Elizabeth's parents 24 years earlier. The locomotive carried a headboard painted with Elizabeth's coat-of-arms and the monogram 'E.P.'. Two Pullman coaches, *Rosemary* and *Rosamund*, formed the core of the special train with *Rosemary* selected as the royal conveyance. Elizabeth's favourite corgi was waiting inside with a footman.

By 1950, it was known that the King suffered from cancer and that the measure of his days was very short. He and the Queen, having

Far left: Princess Elizabeth sounds the locomotive's whistle aboard the celebrated White Train, watched by Princess Margaret and F C Sturrock, the South African Minister of Transport, during the Royal Family's tour of South Africa in 1947. *NRM 95/97*

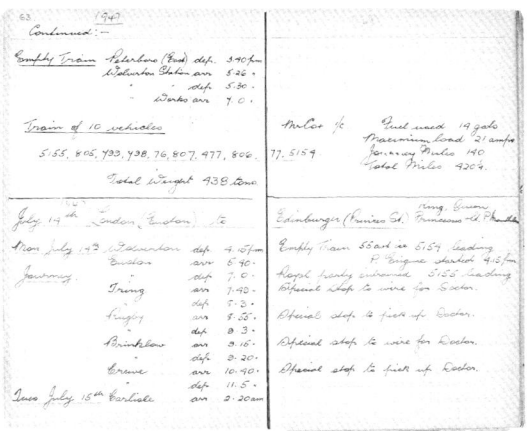

Left: Extract from the Royal Train Foreman's logbook, detailing a journey to Edinburgh on 14 July 1947. The notes on the right show the four special stops made by the train in order to summon a doctor for the Queen, in whose eye a piece of grit had lodged. *NRM 99/97*

accepted that they would produce no male heir, had instead concentrated their efforts on grooming Elizabeth for her role as the next monarch. Their North American tour of 1939 had enabled them to emerge from the chrysalis of their former lives and come to terms with their new roles as King and Queen. Believing that the same experience might be beneficial to their daughter, a similar tour was arranged for the Princess and her husband in 1951. Elizabeth and Philip were provided with a massive Royal Train which also accommodated 125 reporters. Following a similar itinerary to that of her parents, they travelled through many of the major cities in Canada and the United States. Although gruelling, there was also time for fun. Philip enjoyed practical jokes. On one occasion he placed a tin of mixed nuts on his wife's dressing table. When she opened it, a giant imitation snake leapt out at her. On another occasion he was seen chasing her

down the train's corridor wearing a pair of huge false teeth.

The Prince and Princess returned to England to find the King failing fast. However, plans had been made for another overseas tour and they left for Kenya at the beginning of February 1952. Sometime during the night of 5 February the Princess became Queen. On hearing the news of her father's death, she flew back to London for his funeral.

The dead King was carried from Sandringham to lie in state at Westminster Hall, before being taken for burial at Windsor. George VI's funeral combined tradition and modernity. As in 1936, the ex-LNER train was commandeered. The locomotive pulling the train was ostensibly *Windsor Castle*, the same engine which had taken George V to his final resting place, but was revealed to be in reality *Bristol Castle* which

Right: Princess Elizabeth, together with her pet corgi, board the Royal Train at Kings Cross Station, 1949. *NRM 496/83*

Far right: The Queen hugs Princess Elizabeth on her return from her North American tour of 1951. The young Prince Charles stands next to Princess Margaret. *NRM 96/97*

had been renamed for the occasion in an effort to preserve tradition. Again, crowds lined the Windsor streets as the King's body was conveyed on the traditional gun carriage by officers and ratings of HMS *Excellent*. In life, George had believed in observing strict punctuality, and in death he was not let down. As the coffin arrived at St George's Chapel for the service at precisely 2.00 p.m., the ordained two-minute silence fell, exactly as planned. Afterwards, and for the first time, the Royal Family had elected not to return to London by train, driving back instead, but special trains were arranged to convey the large numbers of guests who still required transport.

The old King was dead and the times were changing rapidly. However, Elizabeth was devoted to her father's memory and made it known that she wished for as little change as possible. This desire to preserve the memories of happier days extended to her Royal Train. The wartime saloons would remain in use for almost 40 years, and it would not be until the Queen's Silver Jubilee that the train would evolve once more.

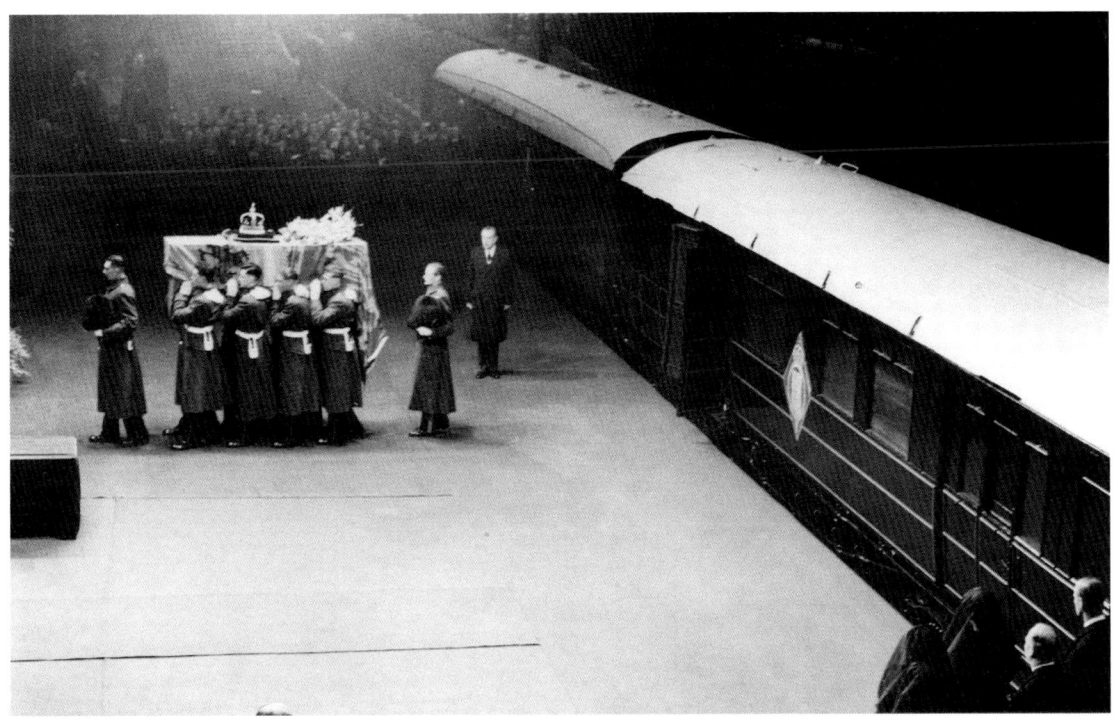

Pall bearers at King's Cross Station walk away from the LNER Royal Train which had brought George VI's body from Sandringham to London to lie in state at Westminster Hall, 11 February 1952. *NRM 91/97*

QUEEN ELIZABETH II
the myth and reality of the Royal Train

More exotic, more opulent, more glamorous and more unattainable than the *Orient Express* of film and literature: this is the public perception of the Queen's most fascinating conveyance. Its attraction is heightened by the fact that no amount of money will buy even the richest and most curious passenger a ticket: a trip on the Royal Train is by Her Majesty's invitation only. In the final years of the twentieth century, the once-impregnable mystique of the monarchy has been somewhat compromised, but the Royal Train remains imbued with the mystery and glamour attributed to the accoutrements of royalty since ancient times. The secrecy which surrounds the intended movements of the Royal Family is necessary to protect them from security threats, but it is the intention of this chapter to raise the corner of the opaque veil which shrouds this much-misunderstood entity. An examination of newspaper reports over the years reveals that a mythology has sprung up around the train: it is reported that the control room contains enough equipment to resemble that of a spaceship, that there are escape hatches in unlikely places in the event of hijack, that the gadgetry is inspired by popular spy films, and that the body of the train is armoured against missile attack. Estimates of its running costs veer wildly from £2 million to £7 million a year.

The truth is less outrageous but nonetheless equally compelling. The Royal Train of today is a sleek, streamlined, functional, thoroughly modern, but still recognisable descendant of its Victorian and Edwardian forebears. The wheel has turned full circle and the British railway industry of the late twentieth century with its newly privatised and grandly named companies, each serving a particular region of the country, bears a passing resemblance to the railway system of earlier decades. However, the era has long since passed when each company would lovingly design and construct a royal saloon and deem it a signal honour if the King or Queen would grace their lines. Although in the 1950s a nursery car was constructed for the infant Prince Charles and Princess Anne, and a new royal dining car and saloon were added for Royal Household members, the 1940s GWR train remained in use into the 1960s, and it was not until the Silver Jubilee year of 1977 that the old LMS wartime saloons were finally given over to preservation (the Queen Mother's saloon being displayed in the NRM). The present royal fleet of 14 vehicles is housed at Wolverton Depot, the traditional resting place of the Royal Train since the nineteenth century, and overseen by Railcare. Four new saloons were constructed at Wolverton in 1977: two royal saloons to replace the outdated wartime saloons, a staff car and a power car. In the decade that followed, the other royal vehicles (existing carriages brought into royal service in 1977) were upgraded.

Although there are several vehicles which may be called into use, the minimum number of

Opposite: The Queen and the Duke of Edinburgh bid farewell to onlookers as the Royal Train departs from Sunderland Station, 29 October 1954. *NRM 97/97*

vehicles required to run the train, the identity of the royal passenger, the numbers of the household accompanying them, and the length of the journey are some of the deciding factors in the assemblage of the train. Typically, however, between five and nine vehicles are employed, and two trains can be assembled should the need arise. This occurs only rarely, since the staff of the various royal households convene to compare commitments. Much pre-planning goes into the preparation of a royal journey, and it is after this initial meeting that

the formation and scheduling of the train is decided. The cost of royal travel arrangements had previously been met by the Department of Transport, the Ministry of Defence and the Foreign and Commonwealth Office, but from 1 April 1997, it was agreed that these costs would be met from a single grant-in-aid of £19.5 million, to be administered by the Royal Household. Of this amount, the Royal Train is allowed just £1.9 million (at the time of writing). In addition, a Royal Travel Office, based at RAF Northolt in Middlesex, was

The Prince and Princess of Wales enter Edward VII's 1902 LNWR saloon on a visit to the NRM, 12 November 1981.
NRM 755/81

established to determine the most cost-effective method of travel, while still ensuring that members of the Royal Family journey in a manner appropriate to their status as representatives of the nation, and that adequate security measures are maintained.

The present Queen's requirements for her living accommodation are markedly different from Victoria's palatial expectations. The era of silk-covered walls hung with valuable paintings, and furniture upholstered in brocade has long since vanished. The modern Royal Train more closely resembles a standard hotel and that is the role it now plays, the quarters used by the Queen and the Duke of Edinburgh being very modestly furnished. Both bedrooms are accompanied by bathrooms with accessories purchased from ordinary high-street shops; the study and dining room are pleasantly furnished but functional. The Prince of Wales has adopted two saloons for use by his children and household. Interior designers and Palace advisors are probably consulted over the decor of all the main saloons,

R.T.

The Royal Train

MENU

Fresh Asparagus with Hollandaise Sauce

Medallions of Lamb
Choice of Vegetables
Macaire & Boiled Potatoes

Deep Filled Apple Pie With Cream

Coffee

Thursday October 3rd 1996

Menu provided for the Princess Royal on her journey from King's Cross to Doncaster Europort on 3 October 1996. The Princess entertained members of the Animal Health Trust en route. *Railcare*

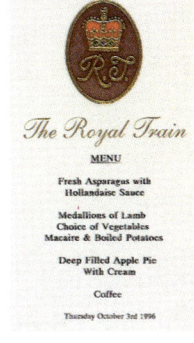

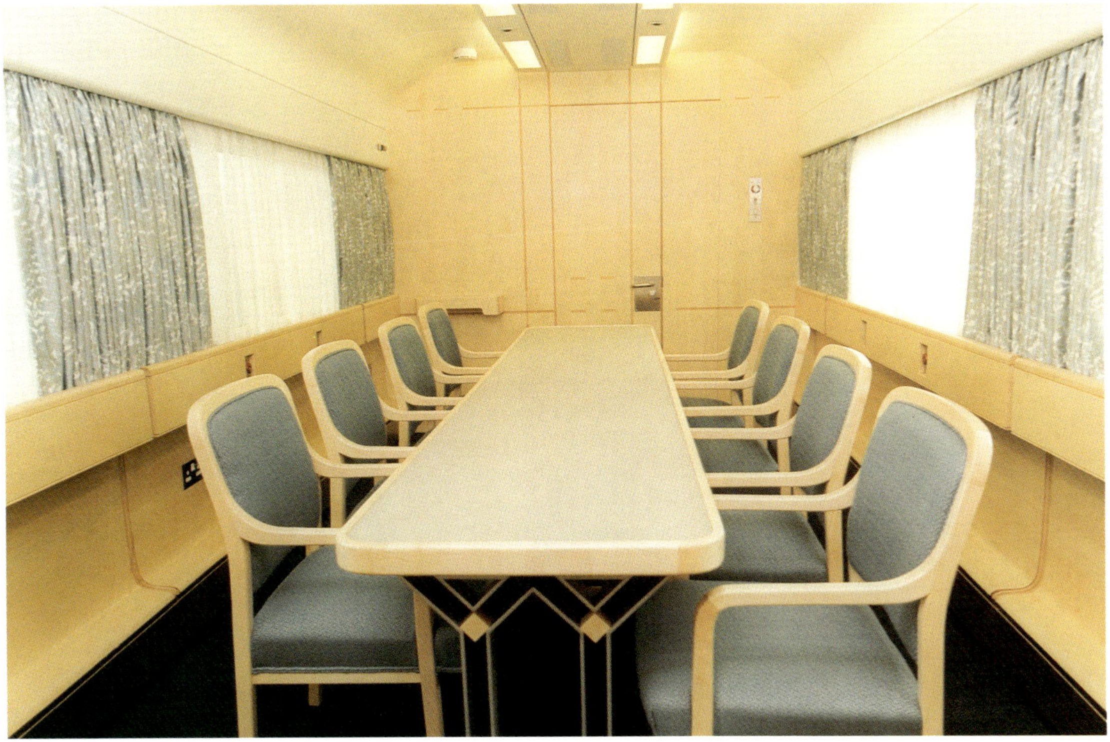

The Queen's dining car on the modern Royal Train. Designed by Sir Hugh Casson, the interior is panelled with sycamore. *Crown Copyright*

and since he is known to possess marked aesthetic tastes, it is likely that the Prince has taken a keen interest in the interior design of his own carriages. His saloons are said to be less spartan than those belonging to the Queen and the Duke of Edinburgh, but are by no means lavish and are characterised by personal possessions and small mementoes presented to him on engagements. He has the use of a study and a dining room, attractively furnished in muted shades. The present Queen has no objections to taking meals on a moving train, in contrast to Queen Victoria, and the Royal Train

contains kitchens fitted with the apparatus found in ordinary rail vehicles. The menu reflects the palates of the passengers, but is simple rather than epicurean.

The Royal Family is known for its frugality in its daily domestic arrangements, and this economy has resulted in the evolution of the unusual custom of airing the beds with footwarmers once used by Queen Victoria and her household. Fred Beeken, who began working on the Royal Train as an electrician based at Doncaster Works during the Second

Right: Chef Martin Carter of European Rail Catering prepares sausage rolls in the Royal Train kitchen. The cooking facilities in the kitchen are identical to those provided in ordinary passenger trains. *Railcare*

Far right: A shopping list of food purchased in a Wolverton grocery on 10 July 1969 for the preparation of staff meals on the Royal Train. *NRM 98/97*

World War, recalled the attempts at economy even in the first days of the Queen's reign:

In the early days we always had the full train out because . . . there were so many hangers on, staff, this and the other . . . and I'll tell you this, the Queen used to have to pay the railway company to hire the train, and she also had a railway ticket. And I've seen her hand the ticket from herself to the footman . . . then he'd hand it to the railway officials. . .. It was one of those times when the train was on a longish journey and we were all sat at our table in the back end of the train and it had never been known in the history of travelling in the royal train that any of the royal family would leave the saloon and walk through the train . . . I just happened to . . . look up . . . in walked Philip with Charles. Charlie would be about this high, holding his hand you see. Well, I mean we all stood up, we'd never known anything like it before.

The Duke of Edinburgh wanted to show his son over the train, but Beeken guessed that after the Duke saw the numbers of staff and

Uniform items worn by staff members of the Royal Train today. Blue and maroon ties indicate the wearer has completed 'ten Royal Train journeys or two years service directly linked to Royal Train activities'. The black tie is worn by Wolverton staff members, and the green Associate tie by those who assist in maintaining and operating the train. Special blazer patches, tiepins and cufflinks are also worn. *Railcare*

company representatives 'that were wining and dining, . . . he must have thought I'm paying for all this, and the next time there was anything like it they were all missing'[1].

Although ornate Victorian ideas of decor are eschewed in the modern Royal Train, its status is subtly underlined by the continuation of several traditions. Royal crests and emblems are in evidence on the tableware and in other locations. The notepaper is headed by a crown embossed on a regal gold and purple tablet, and a ghostly outline of the 1903 LNWR Edwardian saloon overlays the arrangement of the modern saloons, for it has been found that the placements of furniture devised nearly a century ago still works best today. The paintings hung on the walls are mostly gifts made to the Royal Family over the years, which have been specially selected for display.

Royal Train stationery, for use by members of the Royal Family and their households. *Railcare*

The staff of the Royal Train

The baton of Queen Victoria's valued G P Neele has been handed over in an unbroken line down the years to foreman after foreman, and it currently resides with C D Hillyard. Mr Hillyard's duties vary little in nature from that of his nineteenth-century counterparts, since it is his task to coordinate and personally oversee the maintenance, housekeeping and servicing arrangements on the train while it is running, and to liaise between members of the Royal Household and those who staff the train. In essence, it is his job to see that the work of the Royal Court proceeds uninterrupted and that the passengers receive an efficient and unobtrusive service throughout the journey. Mr Hillyard worked as electrician on the Royal Train for 17 years, before being recommended for this senior position on the retirement of his predecessor, Stanley Butler.

Staffing the Royal Train with stewards, tradesmen and chefs is usually achieved through

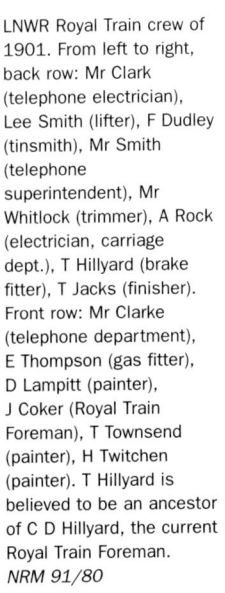

LNWR Royal Train crew of 1901. From left to right, back row: Mr Clark (telephone electrician), Lee Smith (lifter), F Dudley (tinsmith), Mr Smith (telephone superintendent), Mr Whitlock (trimmer), A Rock (electrician, carriage dept.), T Hillyard (brake fitter), T Jacks (finisher). Front row: Mr Clarke (telephone department), E Thompson (gas fitter), D Lampitt (painter), J Coker (Royal Train Foreman), T Townsend (painter), H Twitchen (painter). T Hillyard is believed to be an ancestor of C D Hillyard, the current Royal Train Foreman.
NRM 91/80

a similar process of recommendation, or by internal application and security vetting. To obtain a place as staff member of the Royal Train is a matter of pride to those concerned, and indicates a high level of professional achievement. The personal qualities required are discretion, and the ability to be both confident and unassuming whilst serving on board.

Since this group of people need to work so closely together, they have evolved a professional vocabulary which provides them with discreet descriptions for the unusual requirements of their work. One of the most commonly used and striking terms is the habit of referring to members of the Royal Family or distinguished visitors using the train as 'principals'. This theatrical term enhances the sense that the staff members are the unobtrusive, well-schooled supporting players, whose work enables the Queen and her family to enact the major roles they have been assigned.

The crew of the Royal Train in front of the *Prince William* and *Prince Henry* engines in 1995. From left to right, back row: J Best (electrician), G Potts (deputy vehicle builder), A Bavington (plumber), M Booden (fitter), J Tustain (deputy electrician), S Ratcliffe (deputy fitter), E Burgess (deputy painter). Front Row: G Garlic (senior electrician), P Richardson (vehicle builder), M Corbett (depot manager), C D Hillyard (Royal Train Foreman), D Grace (trimmer responsible for coach interiors), T Beechey (painter). *Railcare*

The confines of the Royal Train also oblige the Royal Family to coexist more closely than normal with members of staff, who are often agreeably surprised when some of the myths about royalty are dispelled. Fred Beeken expressed his feelings thus:

You know they're just like anybody else. I mean as long as you respect them and say "Yes, Your Majesty" first and then its "Ma'am" after that . . .. This is what amazed me when I said I'd have the job and went away on the first trip, come back, they [people back home] all came up and said, "What was it like? What was it like?" You know they were frightened. They thought they were made of gold or something like that, as if they weren't human beings.[2]

There were familiar scenes of family life too. On one occasion, Beeken recalled, two small children, Prince Charles and Princess Anne,

The Queen Mother smiles at Chris Hillyard, Royal Train Foreman, as she and the Duke of Edinburgh dismount at Tattenham Corner to attend the Derby, 7 June 1997. *Inspector Michael Foster, British Transport Police*

came running past him through the restaurant car, greeted him politely, and pattered into the 'Old Queen's' carriage (part of the usual Royal Train until 1953, in which they were not allowed to play). A moment later, an annoyed Princess Margaret came after them in pursuit, asked Fred if he had seen them, and disappeared into the adjoining saloon where, 'there was howling and she's . . . giving them a right talking to and fetching them back into their saloon, you know, where they should be'[3].

Just as Neele and his staff were required to provide any service required by Victoria and her family, the present foreman and his colleagues continue that role for today's Royal Family: for example, by answering a principal's query about the cricket score in the Ashes tournament played between England and Australia in 1997. However, many of the archaic practices have been discontinued over the years as the need for them no longer arises. One of the major changes concerns the staff members themselves, who are today required to be more flexible and multiskilled than before.

The special service performed by the Royal Train crew is recognised by the present Royal Family, just as it was by their ancestors. As G P Neele became a familiar sight to Queen Victoria and King Edward VII, it is very likely that the current foreman has made a similar

The Prince of Wales with Leslie Charlesworth, fitter to the Royal Train, on the occasion of his retirement in March 1995. *Leslie Charlesworth*

acquaintanceship with the present Queen and her family. The custom of rewarding long and dedicated years of service is also maintained. Norman Pattenden, the Royal Train Officer who manages the operational aspects of running the train, has been awarded an MBE, whilst Stanley Butler, Royal Train Foreman from 1967 to 1993, received the Royal Victorian Medal. Several members of staff have also been presented with mementoes by individuals such as the Prince of Wales, and some are occasionally invited to the Queen's garden parties at Buckingham Palace.

Operation: Royal Train

The working of the Royal Train falls under the remit of five companies, a very similar arrangement to those made between different railway companies before the nationalisation of the industry in 1948. Ownership of the train rests with Railtrack, but its operation, engineering support and the overseeing of its maintenance is handled by the English, Welsh and Scottish Railways company. As of old, a special timetable is prepared to show the running times of the train, and knowledge of an

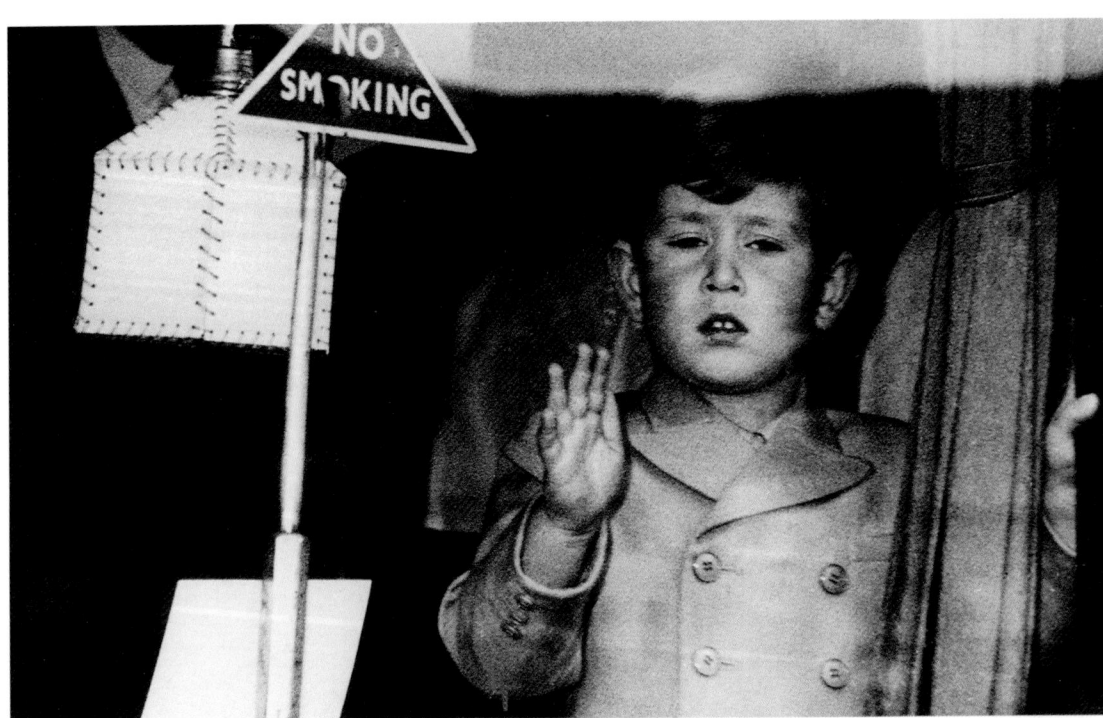

Prince Charles, aged 3, waves to onlookers from the royal saloon, before the train departs Aberdeen for London, 16 June 1952. *NRM 497/83*

impending journey is still on a 'need-to-know' basis. The practice of employing a pilot train was discontinued some time ago, as was the tradition of laying out a red carpet and dressing a station to celebrate the arrival of a principal. However, in November 1973, ten workmen were employed to whitewash the walls of Hitchin Station in Hertfordshire in preparation for a visit by the Queen. In strictest security they painted out the graffiti adorning the underpass, and added an elegant black border to the stairs. Any reference to the identity of their royal visitor was made discreetly, by

describing her as 'the lady with the corgis'. Principals are still greeted by the senior member of the participating railway in the region concerned, and today that person is the area manager. European Rail Catering take care of the Royal Train menu, and the Special Movements Department of the British Transport Police maintain a presence, as the police have done since 1842, on the occasion of Queen Victoria's first railway journey. They occupy their own compartment on the train, and keep in constant communication with the local police forces. They are also responsible for

Chris Hillyard, Royal Train Foreman, bows as the Queen dismounts the Royal Train at Tattenham Corner, 7 June 1997. *Inspector Michael Foster, British Transport Police*

keeping a station 'sterile' once it has been searched, by restricting access. As well as accompanying the more routine journeys made by the Royal Train, they are involved in most major events of national importance, such as monitoring the guests arriving by special train at Waterloo for the Queen's coronation in 1952, and by participating in the high-level security arrangements made to protect British and foreign royalty who were arriving for the funeral of the murdered Earl Mountbatten in September 1979.

Despite the many careful precautions in place when the train makes a journey, it is still vulnerable to unforeseen circumstances. One such occasion was in July 1985, when an American couple drove through a level crossing at Morar in the West Highlands, and crashed into the side of the train (which was not carrying any members of the Royal Family at the time), causing minor damage to both vehicles. After the couple explained that in the USA a flashing red light means 'proceed with caution' instead of 'stop' as it does in Britain,

The Royal Train at Teignmouth, South Devon, May 1995. Locomotive No. 47798 *Prince William* heads the train, and No. 47799 *Prince Henry* follows at the back. *Brian Morrison*

the charge of careless driving made against them was dropped. There are also occasions when plans go amiss—there are stories of staff and luggage left on platforms when the signal for the train to depart has been given too early. Fred Beeken recalls an incident at Wolferton Station, when the train had been requested to take the Queen back to London 'for something to do with Parliament'. The doors were just closing, the young Prince Charles standing by his grandmother, when,

[Charles] must have seen this [guard's] whistle . . . next thing we saw was the guard hand him the whistle. Well of course Charlie put it in his mouth, engine went 'toot' recognising it, sets off . . . Queen Mother bent back double laughing her socks off, and the next thing I see is the guard running up the platform and I open a door and he jumps in . . . he nearly missed the train.[4]

Between 30 and 35 journeys are undertaken by the Royal Train each year, and these are scheduled to slot in with the workings of

The Princess of Wales proudly displays her baby, Prince Henry, on her arrival at Southampton Docks station on 7 August 1985, en route to HMY *Britannia. David Lunn*

ordinary trains. In the early days of the Royal Train, the senior members of the Royal Family would most often make use of the train. Today, the Royal Train is open to all members of the Royal Family who require its use. In recent years, apart from the Queen and the Duke of Edinburgh, the Queen Mother, the Prince of Wales and his two sons, the Princess Royal, her children Peter and Zara Phillips, the Duke of York, the Duchess of Kent, the Duke and Duchess of Gloucester, Princess Alexandra and her husband the Hon. Angus Ogilvy, and Viscount and Viscountess Linley are listed as having completed journeys on the train. Two locomotives head the train, housed at Crewe, and after repainting and revarnishing at Wolverton in May 1995, the newly claret-

coloured engines were retitled No. 47798 *Prince William* and No. 47799 *Prince Henry*, after the sons of the Prince and Princess of Wales. It is known that both young princes take a special interest in the Royal Train, and the log for 7–8 April 1996 tells us that while they were travelling from Slough to North Queensferry with their father, Prince Henry took a tour of the train and locomotive during a recess stop, perhaps because on this occasion the engine hauling the train was his namesake.

Throughout its history, the Royal Train has had a role to play in sad as well as happy royal occasions. In the early hours of the morning on Sunday 31 August 1997, Diana, Princess of Wales was tragically killed in a car crash in

Alec Bath, Operations Director of European Passenger Services displays the combined Eurostar and Royal Train crests on a plaque presented to him by Railcare, after the inaugural journey of the Queen on the Eurostar train through the Channel Tunnel on 6 May 1994. C D Hillyard, the Royal Train Foreman, stands beside him. *Paul Whiting*

Paris. She was 36 years old. In the first days of her marriage to the Prince of Wales, she had been a well-known passenger on the Royal Train, though after the birth of her sons she became a less familiar sight. She told a staff member that she no longer used the train so frequently since she preferred to complete her engagements in a day, allowing her to return home to spend time with 'her boys' in the evenings. On Saturday 6 September 1997, the Royal Train was assigned a poignant part in the funeral arrangements of the Princess, for it was asked to take her children from London Euston to Long Buckby Station in Northamptonshire, to attend her burial at nearby Althorp, the Spencer estate. Once again, the Royal Train was able to prove its worth, not only by the speed of its response to the unexpected call for its services at short notice, but also by providing much-needed privacy following the ordeal of a public funeral.

The future of the Royal Train: mainline or sideline?

The Royal Train has survived since its beginnings as an innovative but misunderstood mode of conveyance in the 1840s, through the period when the railways thundered unequalled through the colonies of the Empire, and into the present day, when its existence is challenged by the helicopter, the airbus and the motor car. It may be seen by some to be a drain on limited funds, but the Royal Train still has a useful role to play in the affairs of state. The inaugural journey by members of the Royal Family

through the Channel Tunnel in 1994, for example, may be the beginning of an extended brief for Royal Train activities. In bygone days, the SER's Continental Royal Train would be on hand should Queen Victoria, King Edward VII or King George V need to travel about Europe. Today, the Tunnel makes it possible for the British Royal Train to travel anywhere the gauge allows it to do so. Cities such as Munich, Lille, Lyons, Paris and Brussels can be as easily reached as Glasgow or Edinburgh. It has the advantage over other forms of transport in that it can offer self-contained private facilities, and perform city-to-city journeys in one fluid motion without interruption. Like the old Royal Yacht, HMY *Britannia*, the Royal Train also acts as a facility for state hospitality.

Since the construction of the first royal saloon over 150 years ago, the world has changed out of all recognition. To survive, the Royal Train has had to adapt itself to changing technologies, to the changing needs of the Royal Family and to changes in British society and culture. As the century draws to a close, there are some who question the survival of the Royal Family beyond the lifetime of the present Queen. As the Royal Train travels into the next millennium, its future may well be tested by the needs of a monarchy which has itself evolved. However, the advantages presented by the Royal Train to maintain national prestige and facilitate state affairs are considerable and unique. To those who debate its purpose, the Royal Train may well reply by adapting itself again to meet these new challenges.

SATURDAY, 6 SEPTEMBER 1997

LONDON (EUSTON) TO LONG BUCKBY

Euston	Depart	12.30
Watford Junction	Pass	12.57
Tring	Pass	13.11
Milton Keynes Central	Pass	13.32
Northampton	Pass	13.51
Long Buckby	Arrive	14.03

Timetable for the journey by the Prince of Wales, Princes William and Henry, and members of the Spencer family from London Euston to Long Buckby in Northamptonshire on Saturday 6 September 1997. The Royal Train took them to attend the burial of Diana, Princess of Wales at Althorp. Following traditions established in Queen Victoria's day, the precise timings for each stage of the journey are laid down. *Railcare*

NOTES

Abbreviations
RA   Royal Archives, Windsor
JQV Journal of Queen Victoria

Queen Adelaide: royal rail pioneer
1   Letter from Queen Adelaide to Queen Victoria, 20 July 1840, RA Y1/14

Queen Victoria: the customer is always right
1   Letter from Queen Victoria to her uncle, King Leopold of Belgium, 14 June 1842, RA 790/51
2   JQV, 13 June 1842, RA
3   *The Times*, 14 June 1842
4   *Ibid.*
5   *Ibid.*
6   Norman Pattenden MBE, 'Victoria to Netley—A Royal Journey', *South Western Circular,* Part I, Vol. 10 No. 5 (January 1996), p.106
7   George P Neele, *Railway Reminiscences* (London: McCorquodale & Co, 1904), p.479
8   JQV, 23 November 1880, RA
9   JQV, 11 February 1888, RA
10 Neele, p.517
11 Neele, p.523
12 Neele, p.484
13 Neele, p.485 (incident took place on 20 May 1868)
14 Neele, p.489
15 Neele, p.418
16 Neele, p.528
17 Letter from Queen Victoria to her daughter Empress Frederick of Prussia, quoted in James Pope-Hennessy (ed.), *Queen Victoria at Windsor and Balmoral. Letters from her granddaughter Princess Victoria of Prussia, June 1889* (London: George Allen and Unwin Ltd, 1959), p.49
18 Neele, p.477
19 JQV, 2 March 1882, RA
20 'God Save the Queen. A GWR ode for Diamond Jubilee Day', *GWR Magazine,* Vol IX No. 8 (June 1897), p.93

King Edward VII and the golden age of Royal Train travel
1   Neele, p.374
2   Neele, p.318
3   Telegram from Edward VII to his mistress, Alice Keppel, 4 April 1900, quoted in Richard Hough, *Edward and Alexandra: Their Private and Public Lives* (London: Hodder & Stoughton, 1992), p.203

King George V: a new role for the Royal Train
1   Diary of King George V, 14 July 1903, RA
2   Diary of Samuel Maun, stationmaster at Windsor 1903–1925, quoted in C R Potts, *Windsor to Slough. A Royal Branch Line* (Oxford: Oakwood Press, 1993), p.97

Queen Elizabeth II: myth and reality of the Royal Train
1   Joan Grundy (collector) and Jennifer Stead (ed.), 'A Doncaster Electrician on the Royal Train. Reminiscences of Fred Beeken', *Old West Riding. A Collection of Original Articles,* Vol. 4 No. 2 (Winter 1984), p.19
2   Grundy and Stead, p.18
3   Grundy and Stead, p.19
4   Grundy and Stead, p.18

Further reading
David Duff (ed.), *Queen Victoria in the Highlands. Based on extracts from Queen Victoria's Highland Journals.* (London: Webb and Bower, 1980)

C Hamilton Ellis, 'Notes on Queen Victoria's Journeys to and from Balmoral', in *Railway Magazine,* 431 (May 1933), pp.34–46

C Hamilton Ellis, *Royal Trains* (London: Routledge & Kegan Paul, 1975)

D Jenkinson and G Townend, *Palaces on Wheels* (London: HMSO, 1981)

Patrick Kingston, *Royal Trains* (Newton Abbot: David & Charles, 1985)